MW00768293

PROMOTION COPY
NOT FOR SALE
FOR MORE INFORMATION PLEASE
CONTACT THE PUBLISHER AT
sales@pjpublishing.org

Sandra Jackson's

35 Tips for Caregivers
A Boomer's Guide to Caring for A Loved One

Good hints peppered with common sense

COPYRIGHT © 2008 by PJ KELLY & Associates, Saugus, Massachusetts 01906

Published by PJ KELLY & Associates, Saugus, Massachusetts, 01906.

Library of Congress Cataloging-in-Publication Data.

Jackson, Sandra.

Sandra Jackson's 35 Tips for Caregivers, A Boomer's Guide to Caring for A Loved One
Good hints peppered with common sense

Includes index for reference materials

ISBN: 0-9675873-5-2

Title: Sandra Jackson's 35 Tips for Caregivers, A Boomer's Guide to Caring for A Loved One

Cover Design: PJ's Publishing and Kistler Printing
Book Design: Jazz Martin
First Printing
Manufactured in the United States of America.
Kistler Printing and Kistler Printing Graphic Design.

Photographer: Tony Irving

Sandra Jackson's 35 Tips for Caregivers, A Boomer's Guide to Caring for A Loved One is a PJ's Publishing book, published by PJ KELLY & Associates.

CONTENTS

Dedication

I am truly blessed to have the health and opportunity to share my knowledge. I am blessed to have had contact with so many who have guided and taught me so much.

To 'my girls'
Thank you Mom for loving me without question, wrapping me in encouragement and strength when I need it, and always pointing me forward.

And thank you Margreat, my sister and best buddy, for showering me with love and friendship. Thank you both for being my steady, unabashed cheerleading squad.

And to 'my guys'
Thank you Daddy, your love and patience has never shown wear or tear and your wise words and endless aphorisms keep me strong.

To John, my husband, my love, my friend. Your unwavering support, inspiration, truth, and boundless energy are gifts you give to me every day. You have always been and will always be my soul's true mate.

And to all my children,
Brandon, Crystal, Elbita, Minerva, David, Ashley, Yessinnia, Khalid, and Khalilah. I love that you all love me and appreciate my old fashioned ways!

This book is dedicated to each of you, my brother Bill, and to the rest of my family, my friends, and to the memory of my Grandmothers Anna and Margreat.

Acknowledgment and Recognition

I'd like to acknowledge and thank our dedicated journalists, radio personalities, and newscasters for their research and stories that have enriched our lives and expanded our minds. We all carry with us the results of your findings and have absorbed your good work.

Recognition is in order for the amazing work done every day by caring health professionals across the country and particularly to the surgeons in the trauma unit in Colorado.

I had the honor to work for a group of doctors at Swedish Medical Center in Englewood, Colorado, whose mission was to heal, treat, and console. Day and night, no matter the emergency, they were dedicated to each individual who needed their care. I have the utmost respect for Dr. Michael Crone, Dr. Emmitt McGuire, Dr. Sue Slone, and Dr. Burt Katubig.

INTRODUCTION

Hey Baby Boomers, all 70+ million of you (and everybody else out there faced with this new and exciting challenge you didn't know would come your way) listen up: Things and times have changed!

It's not that we don't know about change or challenges. I mean after all, most of us have gone through some particularly defining moments (think wars, Woodstock, protests, and let's put it out there--just plain growing up). With all those moments, I believe most of us who find ourselves in a caregiving role are stuck in time (the good old days) thinking that we've still got it all in front of us and that no matter what's going on around us, nothing has really changed. Well my fine, finally-got-the-money-in-the-savings-account, vacations-are-on-schedule, and we're-looking-better-than-we-ever-thought-we-would-at-this-age friends, times have changed. In our oh-so-organized, clothes lined up for the spring or winter, Uncle Sam-paid-in-full, season tickets in-hand, well-planned lives, things, whether we want them to or not, change very quickly.

Let's say you're going along in your regular, normal sort of a day with most of the routine better than usual and a few things worse than before. Then wham — change hits you in the face! It could be a telephone call, a knock on the door, or the realization you're needed that tugs at your heartstrings after a visit with a loved one. You will realize in a minute's time that addresses might need to change or the total independence and freedom of movement enjoyed by me is not guaranteed to carry to the next day or even the next second! You — we — are needed.

When change happens, there's a domino effect that's set in motion and a readying starts for what I call the *after-change*. It will involve you and your full attention. It will also consume your mind and body, as you begin to manage the process of making the necessary changes that need to happen. And, if you don't take hold right now, it will drain you and wring out your spirit. Think: Rule your life.

This after-change is going to be major and might require you to adjust from the once nurtured child to the nurturer or from having a loving, intimate and robust relationship with your mate to spousal nurse-assistant. You might have to go from a newly 'empty-nested' parent to full-time caregiver. And just as the sun comes up everyday and scoots the moon out the way, you can depend on there being an onslaught of even more changes and after-changes that will follow. For example, acting on this new call will mean there are going to be situation changes. The house is going to change, the people in it will change, moods and attitudes will change, schedules will have to change, you'll change the way you speak to your boss, and believe me, you the caregiver and the loved one or patient will see the change. Since we usually don't pay much attention to change as it skips by us on a daily basis, it will appear to come quickly. A co-worker said it simply: everything is fine until it isn't.

You know what else changes right before our eyes? Times. These are truly the best of times for many of us Boomers. Although our fast-growing, aging population is a vibrant, traveling, and exercising lot, to quote a late, musical genius, "change gonna come."

Trust that, as the generation before the boomers lives longer (you've heard the stories, parents 100 years old, children giving care at 80!) someone will probably need our care. We'd better know how to step up to the task and add some levity and common sense to the situation. Caregivers will need to help maintain — or secure in whatever way possible — their loved one's good quality of life.

Now's a good time to set out my record and tell you to dismiss any thoughts of future claims of medical impropriety. I am not a professional home care worker and have the good fortune to have healthy (albeit, as I write, healing) parents, other relatives, and friends. I am not now, have never been, and don't profess to be a healer of any kind. (Okay, so my Grandmother said I inherited my great Grandmothers' talent as a healer but I wouldn't hang out a sign!) I am not a doctor or practicing physician in or of any field, and in this book, I make no recommendation to or for the use, nonuse or viability of any medical program, medical facility, or prescription medication. Any mention of, or reference to, any organization is not intended to discredit and suggestions for use are for your research. This book is not offered to be a medical primer or an alternative to medical care. Please, please, please, always, always, always, speak to the attending physician or medical provider of anyone for whom you provide care in order to determine their needs.

What I've been told I do have is an uncanny sense of order and planning, good common sense, intuition that seldom fails me, and the innate desire to see people live more comfortable and happy lives. Over the past six years, I've lectured to numerous caregivers' groups in different cities and have been known as the caregivers' coach and a coach and inspiration to those who need care. I've studied and cared for people in a number of situations and have always had a genuine interest to discover what works to bring brightness to those who have lost their independence. I've gained this insight from the opportunities I've had to care for people who are or aren't with us any longer. My grandmother was a stroke victim, bedridden and incontinent. I had an aunt I was able to spend time with as she went from hospital to hospice and there were invaluable lessons learned from my mother-in-law's condition, an Alzheimer's patient. I've been there for the major surgeries and minor ailments of my now very healthy parents, and I was on site during caregiving for my nephew (a healthy teenager until surgery temporarily sidelined him). I have also supported the caregiving responsibilities for dear friends and neighbors and have paid close attention to the stories of numerous people who have cared for loved ones as well. I've known good, and bad to horrible healthcare providers and hospital workers whose work or care enlightened me (often unknowingly) by the expressions on their patients' faces, which left no question as to what worked for the patient and what didn't. I took the time to watch, listen, and ask, all the while making mental notes of tips I knew I needed to share.

These are just some of the tips I've garnered, 35 of them, to share with people who are now, or know they will be, giving care. These are tips for you, Boomers, and your friends or relatives and loved ones. I put together these tips to help you put some 'light and lively' back into your life and back into the life of the person who requires your care.

Applying these tips won't make you crazy (because you don't need that right now) and you don't have to do intensive study to get the point of them. In fact, I want you to lighten up. Apply the tips that will work for you and your situation, share the ones that you think will work for someone else, and then relax, knowing that you're doing the best you can for you and your loved one.

Call me! (Well, e-mail me.)

Sandra

Chapter I

TAKE GIANT STEPS

#1 Face the Truth About Caregiving
Be sure you understand what caregiving really is.

You have to face the truth about caregiving. Whether the responsibility of caregiving is old or new for you. It's important you understand you can't take it lightly.

Caregivers make up a huge population that's growing by leaps and bounds every day. You probably have a host of friends and relatives who are, or soon will be, in your same situation and will add to the population of people giving care. Undocumented numbers of this new group of caregivers, mainly boomers, were in the 22 to 40 million range two years ago. Most caregivers are people who, like yourself didn't choose caregiving as a new profession and didn't have time to plan for this new responsibility.

I would say that most caregivers are thrust into caregiver roles and usually unexpectedly, either from calamities of nature, war casualties, accidents, or health problems. There could be a hurricane, a flood, a house no longer comfprtable for an injured or elder person, or maybe a loved one takes a fall down a flight of stairs. People have even been known to get hit by a bolt of light-ning! When something happens to change the life of a loved one, whether for a few days, a few months or for many years, it will also change the life of somebody else — then another caregiver is added to the growing list.

All caregivers learn one thing very quickly: Having to care for someone else is hard work, and not fun. People who are being cared for learn something very quickly, too: Having to be cared for is no fun either.

Let me share some headline news with you. Bob Stein a writer for MSNBC wrote in a recent on-line column that boomers – yes- - boomers, the main group of caregivers or soon to be caregivers— are not as healthy as their parents were at the same age. He went on to say maybe it's because the boomers aren't as active as their parents were, not climbing the stairs as much, are walking much less, and are not doing as much physical labor. This generation called baby boomers has more high blood pressure (could it be tied to the stress of the 21st century?) and obesity than past generations. I say, I guess those 10-mile walks to school in rain, hail, sleet and snow really made a difference for the last generation.

In this fast paced world of ours with conveniences abounding, most of the boomers are taking care of a generation up, a generation (or two) below, and sometimes both (or all three) at the same time. When it's two, it's called by many the sandwich generation. I guess if it's three, we have to refer to it as the triple-decker.

Another headline: "Caregiver's health in a spiraling downward motion." Well, yeah! The national, weekday newspaper, USA Today reported that caregivers have 90% more stress than non caregivers, have 69% less time to spend with family and friends, use more medication, suffer huge weight losses and weight gains, and that the extremely intense duties of caregiving cause deterioration. If you've been giving care, you probably say these statistics are shallow and don't even scratch the surface. I point this out for two reasons: one because you need to make a decision (if you've got a choice) to get to the heart of what's ahead by being truthful about caregiving and what it is; and two, you need to get to the heart of what's ahead by being truthful about caregiving and what it is! Make sure you have a long talk with YOU, asking hard questions and giving honest answers.

What good options are available for the person in need of care? You'll have to ask yourself tough questions, like: Can I undertake this challenge mentally, physically, and financially? Do I want to take on this challenge emotionally?

In order to answer the questions you have to really know yourself and what you can and can't handle physically, mentally, or financially. Whatever your honest and truthful questions are to yourself, here's one answer I want you to remember: the truth is, caregiving is hard work. It's rough territory that can be hard on your mind, your body, your wallet, and your life.

Listen, we live in a crazy, got to be politically correct world that forces us to be less than truthful about our feelings and what we really like and dislike. We're always afraid we'll say the wrong thing in public or have the human resources department looking over our shoulders and questioning us at work. We put up with rude cashiers, have to talk about our accounts with telephone customer service reps who are in countries six thousand miles away, fear and worry about road rage (ours and theirs!) rising utilities rates, and the taxes that are due — and soon.

The truth is, in the world of a caregiver you will have the additional day-to-day duties of visiting, bathing, cooking, feeding, changing someone else's clothes, cleaning up blood, lifting, pulling, pushing, wiping up messes, and did I mention getting some laundry done again because another accident means changing the sheets. You've got people on the phone telling you what more you should be doing while you're still trying to get an IV in just right. And all this comes on top of more college tuition, adjusting to menopause, maybe testing out Viagra, dealing with aching joints, buying and using reading glasses, watching the 401(k)'s losing money again, and just trying to hang on that ladder of success you're still trying to climb while asking for another day off to take your loved one to the hospital.

More truth is, if you're going to do this (and you're going to because you have to, want to, or need to for all the right reasons) just recognize what you're going through personally and remember that caregiving duties will compound the stress and triple the workload.

There's no doubt about it, this has been (or will be) a giant step for you to take. Take another step and make a promise to yourself: don't let caregiving rule your every day, don't let it make you crazy or change your attitude about life (unless you have a bad attitude about life that needs to change, anyway). Do let it change your mind so you're able to approach what needs to be done in a rational way. You can be rational and realistic by taking some time to be still and quiet so good answers come to you. Then pay attention to what's going on and listen to your heart.

My persistent, insistent boomer buddies, please be honest with yourself and face the truth so you'll know when to step up, step aside or step down.

#2 Decide What's Best for Your Situation
Stop, look, listen to your heart to hear what it is saying.

This is the time to really stop, look and listen to your heart to hear what it's saying. Our intelligence will sometimes fail us and our mind might get the best of us and cloud our judgment, but our heart will always tell us the truth.

Unless you live alone, your caregiving duties are not or won't be solely about you and will impact others. Take the time to have regular conversations with everyone who lives in the house with you so that they have the opportunity to share their thoughts and feelings. Either in the beginning or along the way, you will invariably have to set new rules, so make it easy for everyone in the house (children, mates, roommates) to talk about the changes caregiving has brought on and the new situation everyone is in. Children might not like having their routines altered, your attention diverted, or another person living in what they might consider their space. Your mate may understand the need for the care you have to give, but they'll also be concerned about you, your time and attention (or lack thereof) to your relationship with them. Every step of the way, as your caregiving duties become more demanding, always remember that it will be important for all the people who will be affected by the change in your situation to have a chance to speak their minds.

The Stylistics said it best when they sang "...stop, look, listen to your heart hear what it's saying..." What it means is to pay attention to yourself. Remember when our parents and grandparents used to say "If somebody else jumps off the bridge are you going to follow them?" You've been honest, now take the time to be honest about the situation *you're* in, nobody else's home, nobody else's loved ones, and whether or not you can give or continue to give care at your house, in the home of your loved one, or at another facility. Be truthful about where you can give the care, if you can give the care, and when you can give it.

You will also have to be frank about the relationship you have with the person who needs the care and determine if you're the right person for the job. I think it's important to remember who you are and who the patient is, because it will really get down to you, your family, and your loved one being able to live well together or for you and the person who will need your care to be able to relate to each other in order for you to give the best you can. To ease your daily struggles and stresses in your caregiving job, be honest about what your relationship with the person who needs your care has been. From this point forward, keep this tip in mind, repeat it to yourself and hold it as truth: people don't change, situations do.

We're talking personalities here, folks, and personalities and basic character types don't change. Individual personalities dictate who we are, and we've been that person for a long, long time. You might have to address and work out some years-old problems or conflicts. If you have to, to coin a Nike phrase, "just do it." Clear the air and get all feelings out in the open by talking it out because problems won't magically disappear because someone is in need of care. In fact, the problems from the past may become more intense with the stress of the situation you'll both or all find yourselves in. Whatever your relationship with the person in need of care was before this new situation, it will only be magnified now, the good parts, the questionable areas, the bad aspects. If the relationship was sour or bitter because of unresolved issues, it will probably stay sour or become even more so. The personality types of all involved will stay the same; those who are innately demanding will be more demanding; timid may well become more timid; good and kind will remain good and kind. You get the point. It is important for you to help create a good and comfortable living situation. Recognize what you're faced with and what you can manage.

Caregiving duties may last for a short period of time or for more years than you might believe. Consider that the new faces on the Willard Scott's Smucker's segment are even older than those highlighted a few years ago. There are still four or five elders featured who are active and lucid at the anomalistic age of 100-years old. But now, there might be a Mary at 106, or a Jim at 102, a Lucy at 105, and on and on to the lady who is robust and 107 years old. As busy and active these elders are, someone is caring for them in some capacity. Be sincere and make your decision based on the time ahead because it really gets down to your relationship with the person who needs your care and where the care can best be given.

Decide what's best for the sake of the person who needs your attention and care. If you've got people living with you who have problems that might interfere with the wellbeing of your loved one who needs care, be honest about that and the impact it could cause. Alcoholics, sex offenders, anyone with a history of physical abuse, thieves, and people who flat-out dislike the person you care for have no place around someone who can't speak for or defend themselves. Your job is to be honest about the people you love, the people you know, and your situation.

Unless you're in the medical field, you probably aren't or weren't instinctively ready for a caregivers' role and that's okay. You may need to learn to be more direct when you have conversations with your loved one and when you talk to doctors about the needs of your loved one. After you find out what's really going on with the person who needs your care, you'll have a better idea of what you can and can't offer as a caregiver.

Understand that you might have to be flexible about where and how you'll give or continue to give care. The situation could change from care giving in your home to caring for them in their home or possibly having your loved one move closer to you or to alternative housing. Hundreds of elders are moving every year in order to be closer to their relatives and children in order to receive the care they need.

If you decide that an alternate place outside your home is best for all concerned in your particular situation, then please, research, research, research. Your caregiving duties are no less important or necessary to the mental and physical health of your loved one if they are in an assisted living facility or a hospital. And let's be candid because we know bad places exist. There are hospitals under scruntiny and nursing homes that have bad reputations. If you have your doubts for whatever reason about the quality of care, make sure you find another location for your loved one. Rely on your eyes, ears, and nose because they will always give you the truth. The smell of urine, blood and dirt on the floors, hearing patients crying or moaning or seeing many who look poorly kept and over medicated are usually signs that the staff is not concerned about the care of the patients. Make sure the doctors and nurses on staff of any facility you're considering, are qualified, caring and dedicated to the health—better health—and wellbeing of the people who are placed in their care. If your loved one is going to change location to downsize, help them find out about the property (upkeep, the landlord, condominium rules, etc.) and research about the safety of the neighborhood. Find out what you can to make the new situation good for your loved one. Trust your intuition to make good decisions. Also keep in mind that you want to be able to get there for regular visits and that others in the family and friends of your loved one will want to be able to get there, too.

It's a new day in terms of what's available in choices for different care facilities. If you or the person who will move to the facility are concerned about the ethnic makeup of the center, you can probably find one that will meet their needs and yours. There are now facilities designed to suit elders' preferences and ethnic backgrounds from having staff and other patients who speak their language to familiar menu choices for food and recreational activities and music geared to the patients' wants. If your loved one would be more comfortable in a facility where Spanish or Italian is spoken, where the doctors and staff are African-American or Native American, or where the food is consistent with their ethnicity, that offers what would make them and you feel good, chances are you'll be successful in finding one.

You can give good care from anywhere. Just be aware of what will work best for you and your loved one.

#3 You've Got to Make Taking Care of Business Top Priority
Business and Legalese.

It creeps into every part of our lives these days, the business and the legal stuff that seems to be attached to nearly everything we touch. Don't let the business issues that need to be addressed pile up on the kitchen table or on the dresser. In other words, tackle the business correspondence that needs to be addressed. Don't let mail go unopened or telephone calls unreturned. Take care of it because the business side of caregiving is serious stuff.

I know your schedule is so full it could explode and you with it, but the business at hand has got to be taken care of and taken care of regularly. I know the amount of business correspondence and telephone calls has tripled or quadrupled for you because now you've got your regular business and household to manage along with someone else's. Whatever the decision is on where your loved one will be and where you'll give care, there's business involved in making the changes work best for all concerned. From selling homes to closing accounts and opening new ones, to registering cars and keeping up with hospital, cable, and utility bills, there is plenty of business to take care of.

The bad thing is: all this business. The good thing, it's the 21st Century and you're in luck! There are millions of caregivers in this country who have paved some rough roads to get new legislation passed to insure better health coverage. There are also groups and organizations in nearly every city and tomes available that are filled with information you need to help direct you to the nearest office that can help you take care of your business. I'm no expert on the legal and financial aspects, but I know enough to know that it's of utmost importance for you to take care of it and it just makes good common sense. It's easy to get caught up emotionally when we're giving care for someone, but the business side of caregivng has to be kept in the forefront, too. Give it its importance because if you don't, you may lose out on services and money already in place to help you pay bills, get better results, manage, and cope.

With the explosion of the needs of caregivers numerous services and laws have been enacted and developed to help take care of the business of caring for your loved one and laws to govern you in your role. The available services are bountiful and support can be found in unlikely places. You can find the assistance you need by surfing the Internet, reading newspaper articles and books, tuning into PBS television programs, or visiting organizations in your neighborhood.

Several facilities have been set up across the country with dedicated and patient people who are ready and able to help you. And many of those people are caregivers just like you who understand your need for their services. If you happen to find someone who grates on your nerves and doesn't quite fit your idea of helpful and patient, call back another time to speak with someone else or find another place that has the same services or can answer the same questions. Don't waste your time speaking to people who are rude or condesending. If you're like me, after taking care of the personal things on your daily itinerary, you don't have time that. Whenever possible, try to develop a relationship with one person, either on the phone or in person if the facility is close by.

There's no doubt in my mind that at times you'll feel like it's you against the world, but remember you're never really alone. There are counseling centers for one-on-one sessions as well as group sessions at many centers for you to participate in to help you cope. Know where to turn for support and make those centers, day activities, and legal services work for you. As the awareness of caregiving expands, there will be more articles dedicated to the growing caregiver population, and more cities will be addressing their needs with seminars, expos, and workshops. Literature is abundant and available. Grants (not loans) are available to help with your financial needs. Take advantage of whatever is obtainable to make your job lighter and keeps money in the pockets of you and your loved one.

In most cities, there are adult day care centers that are designed not only to care for medical needs but also offer activities on a daily basis for the participants. Transportation is usually available to most centers or can be arranged. Call your church, your local YM/YWCA, read the community news sections in your local papers and write down the names of the editors of stories about senior activities so you can be contact them for more information. Local television station managers and program directors may also have contacts and referrals. And call your city's mayor's office for information. You can also call or write the congressperson, councilperson or any other of your city and government officials.

Check for programs that are in your area for elder care, patient care, and caregivers' support. Hospitals will let you know about programs and steer you to volunteers who can lend a hand when you need it. Call a retirement community and speak to the activities' coordinator or the director, check the classified section of the paper or the government council on aging. You may even find a person who is in your same situation and is eager to share information. Ask around and you might be able to help set up a support group of some kind on your street so that neighbors can work together, can pick up calls or stop by periodically to check on these in need. You might even ask for information from someone in the human resources department at your job.

Be able to answer questions and give general information when you make calls and have the answers handy so you'll save yourself time and aggravation. Whenever you can do this -- save time and aggravation -- do it!

#4 Get What You Need By Asking for What You Want
After years of selling cookies and candy for the kids, you can do it.

Dear caregivers, now is not the time to clam up. Not now when you want or need something to help you get through the job of giving the best care you can for your loved one. And I know you need a lot. I've read staggering figures on the amounts of money caregivers spend on a yearly basis, most of which they won't be able to recover. You know how it works: run to the store to pick up a few things for the house on any given day and stop the next day for drug and bathroom items you need. Then there's the supermarket and the take-out restaurants you'll go to that are close to the shopping center that has the blankets on sale, so you might as well stop there, too. Every place you go is asking for you to dig constantly in your pocket until it's empty. When there's only 'happy dust' left there, then you have to rob your piggy bank. In a study done in 2006, AARP says it was estimated that unpaid caregivers provided the equivalent of $350 billion in elder care with an average out-of-pocket cost of $2,400 per year, calculated on the very low side, I'm sure. High or low, that is a lot of out-of-pocket expense!

After years of selling cookies, candy and whatever else schools have begged each of us to sell, you know how to ask for what you want. Maybe you've forgotten how to ask for what you want or feel like you can just take care of it all yourself. Well, you can't. When someone asks if there's anything you need, you say, "yes," stand tall, look them in the eye and then tell them what it is you want or need. Say it then and there, don't wait to think it through or offer to call back and let them know. Say exactly what it is you need. If you need to know what the doctor means when they say a little or short walk is good for a patient, or a small amount of orange juice is fine, or what is not too late in the day to have food — ask. If you need money, a larger home, transportation, a walk-in-tub, a barber closer to home, a manicure in the house, or answers to questions you have, just ask. If you can't get the answers you need from the person you're talking to, ask them who you should ask! While you're doing all this asking, make certain to ask about the Equal Employment Opportunity guidelines in your state that protect caregivers who have to take time off to give care, because caregiving duties shouldn't leave you without protection in the workplace.

This is the time to get in touch with organizations in your area and get handouts with helpful and useful information and get on the first list you see so you're updated about news for caregivers. Call any elder care assistance program in your area or the first two caregiver support numbers you find in the yellow pages or on-line. I have phone numbers for two of the largest national companies. Give them a call. There's Comfort Keepers at (800) 387-2415 and Eldercare Locator at (800) 677-1116. These places may or may not have exactly what you want or need, but they are great references and can provide referrals to help find services in your city. Start there or add them to your list unless you have scores of other numbers you can use instead. The important part is to make the call and ask for what you need and let interested parties know what you want.

Whether it's a rolling bed you need or discount paper towels, latex gloves, have queries on whether or not you can get paid for your caregiving, or about getting car service, have one note pad with general information about your loved one that might be needed. Keep notes of the names of people you speak with, telephone numbers you've been referred to, and as much data as possible on that one sheet or pad. In order to let you know what might be available to you, the people you call will probably need to know patient age, condition, or your city and insurance provider, just as reference points. Having one pad and pencil handy will save you time and frustration.

It doesn't stop with services or products. If (and whenever) you have concerns about the health provider or organization or doctors assigned to and for your loved one or the level of care that's being given, speak up. Don't feel obligated to continue with a doctor who doesn't meet your requirements or one you feel doesn't have the patient's best care in mind or one who doesn't have characteristics that are important to you. Make sure the doctor is one who will treat your loved one as an individual, not treat them categorized by race, age or gender. After convincing my father, who is very active, to change doctors three times in the past five years, I still fight the battle to convince doctors to view him as an individual not their prejudged version of a black male in his seventies.

We all have the right to be treated by a clean, trained, experienced, polite, caring, knowledgeable, professional who is available to answer our questions. Request a different doctor if you feel you're not getting the care you deserve and then define and express what constitutes better care to you. I've known patients to generally fare better and heal faster when they are happy with their doctor. No one can read your mind so you've got to make it a point to ask for what you want.

> **Hint:** If it's hard for you to ask for some of the things you need, maybe a friend or relative can do it for you by putting it in the church bulletin.

Chapter II

CAREGIVING IS HARD WORK
Get some — and accept some! — help

#5 Let People Be Who They Are and Do What They Do
You might have to pay, but siblings, relatives, and friends *want* to help.

You can barely manage the annoyances like you used to and you're doing your best to get it all done. Still, you're just getting by. You might not even have the time or energy to make the calls to get what you want or need for yourself or the person you're caring for. I believe, really truly believe, have encouraged it, and have seen it work: siblings, relatives, and friends want to help. You're going to need the help so ask for it. This is a big tip that wants to be put into practice right away. To do that you'll have to let people fill the needs that have to be filled in their own way, not the way you want them to do it. Try it this way and I believe you'll get help from your friends, relatives, and siblings. Let me clarify this so there's no mistake: you've got to let people be who they are and do what they do. Everybody wins when you let go of some of the control and stand back and let help come to you.

Whenever I speak to caregivers I'm asked to address the number one problem counselors encounter, which is how to get caregivers to take better care of themselves. I know it feels like you're on your own but the truth is you've got friends and family members who want to help. They say they will, but then they don't. This can be a cause for a source of anger and resentment from too many caregivers who say people won't help them or won't do what they ask them to do. Maybe it's because we tend to ask people to do things they just can't do or aren't able to do. We take them out of their comfort zones and then they can't respond and may even disappear when we need them the most.

Here's a prime example of what I'm talking about. My friend April's mother had surgery not long ago and she said she did everything to try to get one of her sisters to share some cargiving duties. She'd asked her to stay with their mother while she did some shopping or went out just to have time alone and take a break. Her sister called to talk to me about it and told me April was asking her to do things she couldn't do. She also said, of course, she really wanted to help her sister and do things for her mother. Unfortunately, she admitted she felt she couldn't be left alone with their mother because she wouldn't know what to do if something happened or there was an emergency. She's the type of person who can't be left alone with sick people and she gets weak at the sight of blood. Even changing a bandage isn't a job for her.

She is, however, the person who will drive 45 miles to pick up a special request item or to bake a cake made from scratch at 3:00 am if she's asked. I spoke to April and told her I wanted her to try using my tip and let her sister help by doing the things she did best and find other people to stay with her mother when she needed to leave the house for errands, breaks or dates. April started asking her mothers' friends who enjoy visiting to come and visit with her mother while she took care of other things. When the friends weren't available, there were other siblings or relatives who could be called on who liked to visit, maybe visit and talk, or visit and watch television. She gave her sister different chores she could actually manage without a problem. When she did this, she managed to find more time for herself.

You know people who like to do a number of things and have hundreds of skills. Let those friends and family members do what they do to help with the caregiving duties, not what you want them to do. Maybe someone likes to make calls and do research or crunch numbers, let them do that. Do you know somebody who's a CPA, a lawyer, a person who likes to open and sort mail? If these people are friends and relatives (who care about you) they may want to assist in some way with the duties of caregiving not only for you but for themselves, too because we all want to feel that we contribute to good causes. Let those who want to paint, paint, those who want to hang curtains can hang curtains. There are those who are willing to run errands and pick up people who need transportation and drop them off again; and there are those who will cut grass and maintain the yard for you.

Let people who like to visit, visit, and those who want to cook can cook. People want to help. I honestly believe it and I'll say it again. People want to help. But in order to get the help you need, you have to let people do what they do.

Since it's clear we aren't all the same, there are a couple of other things you'll have to keep in mind to really get others to help. (Here's the part where I can almost hear you saying: "Why should I have to ask; they see that I need help. Why can't people just do what I ask them to do?") You're asking yourself, again, why you're the only one with all the responsibility? Well, it's because you caregivers are a special breed. Caregivers take on much and give much in return. There is also the tendency to believe you're the only one who cares, the only one giving, the only one who knows what's needed, and the only one who can do it right (whatever 'it' is). Wrong on all counts. As people open up and give what they can by being who they are, they feel they're sharing in the duties and helping to lighten your load. And they are. You need to remember that and bite your tongue and resist the urge to criticize their efforts. Don't redo what others do for you and don't complain about the way it's done. A bed that's not made to your specific standards is still made just fine. Say thank you and move on.

> **Hint: Never make the giver of any gift of time or self feel unappreciated.**

Okay, sometimes you might have to pay some of the kids and maybe even some of the friends or relatives, but not all of them and not all the time. Put a dollar amount to the task or chore and maybe you'll find it's worth it to pay to have the task done because there's only so much you can do on your own –– only so much any one body can do.

I only gave a short example of siblings at odds when I shared the story about April and her sister, but siblings with different approaches to caregiving or the resurfacing of sibling rivalry for caregiving adults is alive and kicking across the country. If you're caring for a parent or both parents, keep in mind that each of you is going to have to put a cork in the rivalry and work to make life easier for your loved one, and for each other. Remember who you are and what your real personality is in this, too. You are who you are. You've taken on responsibilities the way you wanted to, were asked to, or by luck of the draw, those that just came to you to do. Also in the scenario? You're most likely the only, or the primary, caregiver and you shouldn't have to do it all.

Share the love, share the joy, share the loved one, and by all means, share the work! Find a way to work together, coordinate with each other to get tasks done and make sure all work related to caregiving doesn't fall on you. Again, let people do what they do and be who they are.

If you're the eldest, it may be expected that you'd be the care-giver. If you're the only female or the married sibling, maybe it was expected that you would take over those caregiving duties or open your home to your loved one because birth order and marital status often plays a role in determining which sibling will take on which responsibility. But order and marital status shouldn't mean all siblings aren't responsible to contribute whatever they're capable of contributing. Encouraging all the brothers and sisters to provide for loved ones will ease the burden of the primary-caregiving sibling.

You need help and everybody says to let them know if they can do anything at all. Or they say to call them if you need something. What they don't say is: remember who I am and what I am capable of really doing. Ask your friends and supporters to be specific when offering their services and ask them to do only what they're able to do (make sure it's what they're able to do on their own without them having to rely on anyone else to get the job done). Your busy brother or sister might be people who run companies or have their own business but no time for helping you the way you feel they should. They may, however, have valu-able resources and referrals, or some financial support to send your way! They can refer you to someone or have contacts to reach the person you need or to get you in touch with them to help you get a job done. Have brothers and sisters contribute money, make lots of telephone calls, and visit as often as possible.

Whatever it is that others kick in to help out the situation, they're doing it to provide assistance in their own way. Take it and feel better about it.

This idea of letting people do their thing is a great tip because if you really allow yourself to do it you will get help like you never thought possible. Apply this for the young people in your life (and yes, you might have to pay them or offer bribes, but what the heck, we've been paying and bribing children since they were born) and old alike. Decide what kind of help you need (and friend, you need all the help you can get!) and then call on those people who actually do those things, and are best at them, to give you a hand. You'll feel good knowing there are people coming through for you, lending a hand, and helping you out. Those who are finally able to help in their own way will feel even better knowing they're doing something for you and the person you're caring for, who may be their loved one, too.

What's good to keep in mind is that when you spread the re-sponsibilities around, when you let people offer assistance in their way, you'll find that you don't want or need to be in charge of everything. You don't want to cook all the meals anymore or make all the trips. You'll find that it's possible to get some time and personal space back for yourself when you let others share the load. Put this into practice today and keep it in your mind: you can get what you need by telling the right people and then letting them, do what they do. Be honest about the huge amount of work you have as a caregiver and accept the help.

#6 Remember, Promises Don't Pull Their Weight, People Do
Apply a 'Two-Strike Rule' because three is too many.

You are probably so full of emotions that they're skimming the surface after being pushed up to the top by fatigue, concern, and failing patience. Time is precious and the word of someone should be their bond.

Unfortunately, it comes as no surprise to any of us that sometimes people say they're going to do something and then, for whatever reason, they can't do it or just don't do it. Then, they either give an explanation you listen to or one you don't care to hear. The bottom line is, they didn't come through for you. They do it once and everybody seems to forgive and forget. No problem, we'll say. We go along with them and listen when they say, "next time I'll do it for sure." It's also no surprise when it happens again. That's two strikes. You'll save yourself heartache and time if you let the strikes stop there.

Give a two-strike rule to friends and relatives and business associates, who for whatever reason, do not come through or don't make good on their word the second time. There are too many sources available to you (if you take advantage of them) and people who will help (if you let them do what they do) for you to waste time and energy, and invariably, end up angry because once again, you thought someone would keep their word. Give the benefit of doubt no more than twice, whether it's your mate, a sibling, or a friend. No more than twice and then it's on to another person who <u>will</u> follow-through for you.

Since we probably don't want to quickly place blame on someone else check to see if maybe in all the business of caring for someone else you neglected to do your part. Check yourself first. There are two things you should do to avoid any missteps and to insure a particular chore gets done. The first is of utmost importance. That is, to make certain you identify who gets which chore by assigning the name of the person to the chore so there's no confusion about who was going to take care of it for you. No one can be held responsible if you asked "Anybody" to do it!

For weeks a major project goes undone in the office or at home because it was assigned to one of the three least cooperative and most nefarious people you know. Well meaning, good to the bone, and oh so pleasant to be around, but they're people you can't get anything out of. These are the people who will usually have a good excuse for not coming through and maybe it's because we set them up to fail. We speak to them as though they're a group and hope they'll get the point. Well they don't. We call them Anybody and Somebody, general, nondescript names. When we plead or yell: Will Somebody clean this up? Can Anyone go to the store? I want Someone to make a telephone call for me, we have to realize it may or may not get done.

If you want to get a job done and be able to hold a person accountable, call them by name, speak to them directly and tell them exactly what you'd like them to do. This 'name calling' or calling everybody by their given name goes for all siblings, relatives, and friends.

Next, make sure you communicate all particulars of the task up front. Got a promise for a ride? Decide in the beginning the time and place for pickup and where you need to go. Got an offer from someone to deliver important papers for you or make a trip to the post office? Make sure it's clear when it needs to be done where papers need to be delivered and how anything needs to be mailed. After you're sure you've done your part in being clear about what has to be done and you know who's going to do it, it should get done. If it doesn't, give only one more strike.

You know more people than you think and you'll need to call on them because that 'someone who always lets you down' will not suddenly turn over the proverbial new leaf and follow through. Expand your contact list and call on new people.

Two strikes and they're out. Don't feel bad about cutting off a friend or loved one who doesn't come through for you or make it about love and friendship. Just find someone else the next time you need something done. You've got too much to do so move on to a more reliable person who will get the job done.

Chapter III

Make the Best of a Good Situation

#7 Move Forward With Bits of the Past Close Behind
Let your loved ones with the memories decide which memories to take.

The sheer number of storage facilities seen, coupled with the commercials for trucks that will drop off some extra terrestrial looking pods and pick-up the stuff you have no place for in your house, lets me know we've all got too much junk. What I also know is that what's junk to someone else might be a treasure to you or me. Take for example a rock my mother keeps in her kitchen drawer. It's weighs about four pounds and except that it's abnormally smooth and both ends seem to have been mysteriously sawed off by nature: it's not a spectacular looking piece to me. My mother loves the rock because of the memory she has for the friend who gave it to her years ago after he'd brought it back from a weekend in the country. He'd told her he thought it would be great to use to sharpen knives. I keep a black velvet pillbox hat with a mesh veil that belonged to my grandmother. I'll probably never wear it (mainly because my sister could hardly stop laughing when I put it on one evening) but I always want to see it in my closet.

We all have mementos large and small of earlier days and times in our lives. Because we seldom know the value of what's kept in someone else's closets and drawers, if your loved one is changing homes and moving into yours or you're helping them move from one home to another, find out what holds their heart before tossing everything in the trash. It doesn't have to make sense to you the caregiver, or to anyone else, because it's the stuff of someone else's life we're talking about. Ask your loved one about the photos, the dresses, the hats, the ties, the cups, and the drinking glasses they have, the possessions that you might think aren't worth relocating. Your loved one should be the one to make the decision when possible and within reason (I know that unless you've got a huge amount of private space that your loved one will move into, taking or moving an entire house of 'stuff' might not be plausible). An old ring might look worthless and not as shiny as the 18k you're used to seeing, but its history might shine on in smiles in your loved one's broken or mended heart.

> **Hint: Let the ones with the memories decide which memories will travel with them, which ones they will keep.**

Just think about the things you've accumulated over the years that might not make sense to anyone else: broken jewelry, half-finished art projects, old letters and greeting cards, or a blouse in the storage trunk. Our stuff, everybody's own stuff, is important to them. Even homeless folk have stuff. When we're under the weather or down right sick as can be, we like to have some of our own things around. Sick or well, I like to glance at some of my 'things' and I believe other people like to see their things as well. We don't know why someone might keep a little green saucer they've had around for years, or treasure the picture frame with the factory picture still in it. I once spoke to a woman who was being cared for by her niece and she told me she really missed seeing the little girl in the picture. She'd had the picture and the frame for years but when she moved in with her niece (you guessed it, tossed out by the niece) she didn't see it anymore. She said she hadn't known the little girl, she said she just liked the look on her face and had decided to keep the picture and the frame that it came in.

Let your loved one choose their bits and pieces that will travel with them.

#8 Play the Music and set the Mood
It's a good mood maker and bad mood breaker.

Since I'm talking about stuff, this is a great time to suggest you raid your record, CD, and cassette collection. In case you're wondering why the record and cassette part of that flowed out so easily, it's because a huge part of my cherished stuff is the music. I want you to take yours out, dig through it and find some of your favorites to put on while you're setting up, cleaning out and getting ready to get organized — again. If your loved one has a collection, have them get out some of their favorites and start playing the music to set the mood. You want to set a good mood and energize yourself and your loved one. Set a mood and set up some "chit" and "chat" moments and find out what all the 'stuff' you're moving, storing, or setting up is about. Play music that feels good and the work of clearing out and moving forward might not feel so bad. Give Bob Marley and the Wailers a try. You'll understand and feel him when he says, "...lively up yourself and don't be no drag."

#9 Get ready, Get Set & Get Organized
Make the space you have work for you and yours.

It's always time to make a few changes, but when you're caring for someone, it's a good time to get ready, get set and get organized. Get your house ready for the loved ones who are already there or will soon be there because they need your care. Now is the time, because it's always a good time, to make the space work for you and your loved one. Enlist the help of someone who's up for the challenge (remember, let people be who they are and do what they do) and depending on your loved one, find out what might need to be changed to accommodate them. Little things and small changes make big differences.

Make it easy on yourself, please. Don't make this hard. If your loved one is able to, ask them what might work better. Just sit down in any of the rooms (or one room that needs immediate attention) you think could use an organization re-do to make life easier for you and anyone you're giving care to. Take some time to think it through and write down just what you need to do to reorganize the space and the things that are in it so that the space and traffic flows easily and comfortably in and out of the area. Put on music that gives you high energy and get your mind into those ideas that will help you make the most sense for your new situation. Put on music that has seen you through some unpacking. Diana Ross' 'It's My House' was, and still is, one of my favorite unpacking and setting-up tunes and always lets the creative juices flow. Study the space you have and decide what will work best in a different area of the room or maybe out of the room completely. See it, study it, and then if you're able to and have the time, get busy with some of the changes right then and there. Move what you can, throw out what you need to, and reorganize. Make a list of what you need and where you can get it. Get busy. For things that are already in the house, make an effort to put them where they will be easier to use. For example, if you need a small refrigerator upstairs to keep you from having to make too many trips downstairs (remember those joints, boomers) then get one. You can store juice, milk, water, and if you need to, small snack foods or medication.

If you have to reorganize your kitchen so that it's easier for you the caregiver and the person being cared for, get busy on what you're able to do. If you've got the budget for the pros to come in and build new shelves and closets or relocate a washer and dryer, good for you, and please send me your tips on saving money for major home renovations! Get the workers in there and get the work done.

If you're like many caregivers who find themselves with more people living in the same space they had before more people arrived — and the same amount of money — you will want to reorganize so that the space you're in works better for you, your loved one, and the process of caring for your loved one.

You'll find that simple changes that are within your control work wonders. Steel and plastic shelves are great on landings, basements, and garages. Those plastic shelves can also have a life along with the roll- away drawers. They both work great in closets, under beds or outside the closets — and are useful in holding everything from towels and wash cloths to nightgowns, sheets, and clothes. And because they sit low on the floor and are light-weight and easy to move around, our elders and those who are sick, or sick and tired of reorganizing, have little problem opening, closing and moving them if they need to. I'm not talking about our dream makeovers, here, just better use of space for better organization. If the spices need to be on the bottom shelf, move them, need smaller bowls and plates? — get them. Is the toaster in a bad position, the can opener out of reach, plastic food storage containers reproduced once too often? Change things around, throw out the excess, and get organized. Put your paper products closer to where they'll do you some good and move canned food closer to where you really need it. Whether it's for short or long term, make the space work better for you and your loved one

#10 Personal Space Must Feel Private and Secure
From colors to shoji screens, it can be done.

Create personal space that has a feeling of privacy and security but not isolation and total silence. I know we all have our attachments and penchants, and like most of what drives our lives, it's simply an outpouring of our likes and dislikes. These things, our belongings, can refresh us, relax us, and tranquilize or stimulate our minds and support our well being. We also have definitive choices for colors that attract, calm, or ground us to make us feel at ease or at home.

If you're in a hurry and in a frenzy to get a loved one moved in with you and settled down, either a permanent move from their home to yours or for a temporary stay, the space might need to be more personalized. Even after months or years of caregiving, the personal space of your loved one may have been overlooked. Please, take the time to really look over the space. If a change needs to be made so the space feels more private, secure, and personal then get started on that right now. From new colors for all the walls, or just an accent wall, to changing the direction the bed faces, to adding one or two shoji screens, it can be done and should be done. Making space personal with a feeling of privacy and security will mean the world to the person you care for and ease their agitation, which will inadvertently make you feel better – and I'm all for everyone feeling better!

I remember when my grandmother was in her last year of life and was pretty much confined to the bed. She'd been relocated (downsized) to one room from her home with nine rooms she'd had for about 50 years. After she was moved, her bed was in a family room, which was open to the living room and where anyone was as soon as they entered my aunt's house from the front door. Those creative, single-family house designs in Queens always surprised me.

My Gram was a city woman at heart who could always sleep better when there was plenty of noise and movement going on outside. She liked the hustle and bustle of city life from morning to night. When it was quiet, like it was in this particular section of Queens, she wasn't comfortable in the open, front room. And she shouldn't have been. She told me she if she ever heard someone walking by or just standing outside talking she thought immediately that they were the rough folk because the good people who lived in the neighborhood (which for her meant no less than twenty units per building, four people per unit, sixty buildings on a block) were already inside their homes. If you know New York, think The Bronx and 151st off Broadway in Manhattan as examples of what she knew as amounts of people and bustling activities, her two neighborhoods for more than seventy years, then you can understand that quiet might not be a blessing to your loved one. Gram didn't want total quiet in the house or outside, but she also didn't want to be in clear view in the morning and all day long to the people in the house. I told my aunt that we had to do whatever we could, given where Gram was, the only space in the house where she could be, to make it more private for her.

My aunt and I got busy with creating private space for my grandmother and she guided us every step of the way. We were able to use large screens to define her space. The large front window was blocked with a couple of screens and another screen was used to create a 'wall' so that when someone entered the house, Gram's bed wasn't immediately seen. We put 'stuff' with height and substance (plants she loved, a small dresser with photos of her children, parents, grandchildren, etc.) against the screen blocking the window and two chairs with a small table between them against the created 'wall'. Behind her bed, there was a high window. We put long curtains so it was easy to let the sun in and made the window seem less a threat of entry and added some pictures on both sides of the window. We personalized and gave a feeling of security to her space and made sure she wasn't closed off from conversations and the sounds of everyday living. A bedside table with a drawer for her pocketbook was put by her bed for a radio, her eyeglasses, water, and books or magazines.

> **Hint: We feel comfortable when we can live with and around the stuff we like.**

You can also make space more personal and comfortable with color. Whether it's used on the walls, with the bedding, or with a few pillows or other accessories like flowers, art, or slipcovers, color can make a difference because it makes a definite impact with a visceral effect. Get creative and think creatively while you're watching some of those design shows. A few changes will make a big difference.

Even though there are tons of beautiful colors from which to choose, each one of them doesn't work for all of us. My sister has the unique style to blend and bring a lot of color into her world. I, on the other hand, don't. But if asked — and when I'm feeling high spirited, shades of red from bright to deep and oranges from the dirty side are the colors for me. I like, and live with, terra cotta pots, terra cotta the color, and anything else that reminds me of the earth. I don't like powder and baby blues and wouldn't want to see those colors on walls, sheets, or blankets on a bed I had to sleep in regularly. I'd also be a bit uncomfortable in a room filled with ruffles and lemon yellow. I love flowers in vases and gardens and lemons in my tea, but not on fabric or walls.

While glancing at the MSNBC homepage one day I saw an article by Julie Mulligan, a floral expert. It was a featured article around one of the flower-giving days (mother's day, valentines day, I don't remember which), but it was interesting to read her thoughts about paying attention to the color choices. Some suggestions were to get red for romance and energy, white to suggest innocence or bring on heavenly thoughts, pink for gentle nature and grace, and yellow for friendship and joy.

There is also a longstanding notion that flowers will brighten moods—yours and theirs. You know this already if you've ever received flowers from someone else or stopped at the florist to pick up a bunch of flowers and added them to brighten your room. After more than 50 people who were asked to keep diaries of their emotions and activities were surprised with flowers over a two week period, Nancy L. Etcoff, a clinical researcher, determined the recipients were less stressed.

Although those articles were about color choices and flowers, I've heard that color can set a mood and the affinity for distinct tones usually reflects different personalities. Color is important as a choice and preference for us for design and it seems to have some benefits as far as our moods and perception. Green is used a lot in health care facilities, blue is popular as a calming color and promoting communication, yellow gives energy. I wouldn't suggest using a lot of your time on research unless it's important to find the right energy mix for you if you're interested in Fueng Shui and balance or you're getting into long-term design and have the bucks to spend. When personalizing space for your loved one, go with colors, fabrics, and patterns that make them feel good and colors that look good to them. Those home decorating channels are great for providing hints on doing a lot with a little (little money, patience, energy, or know how). Add the pieces that work in your home and in your space, but always be mindful of creating the atmosphere for a person whose situation has changed. Think back on the great old sitcom, Fraiser, with Kelsey Grammer. Remember the chair his character's father loved and he hated?

Whenever possible, get the input of the people you're caring for and their final decision on what they really like and want around. Large or small changes from a painted wall to a bedspread, new lampshades, or a couple of new pillows, will help create a more soothing and much more appreciated atmosphere.

> Hint: It's just common sense,
> give a little and gain a lot.

As luck would have it, sometimes what needs to be done if you have to care for a loved one in your home or in theirs, might not be as simple or as inexpensive as a few accessories. You might need to invest in new furniture or atleast a new bed. If a bed isn't cozy, rest will be hard to come by for you and your loved ones. At the least, don't let the bed be the problem.

Any furniture should be solid and comfortable. If you've got to get chairs make sure they have sturdy arms, a wide base and are easy to get in and out of. Make the necessary changes so that everyone in the house lives well and sleeps well.

Intergrate treasured possessions into the living space of the person or persons you're caring for and that useful and practical items like a small table close by with a brightly lit lamp, find their way into the space. This will help to encourage and maintain independence. And please do not, I repeat, do not close all doors or turn off all the house lights at night. Tame beds that bite, fix the corners that cut, make space for bedside items, and pick up those carpets or rugs that can trip them and a newly tired and exhausted you!

If a television is nearby and the remote control is not, be careful about turning on day-long news and movies. A person on medication, bedridden, an older person who naps frequently, or a person whose mind is not as sharp as it used to be which is half the world, can drift in and out of sleep and might be startled by sudden bursts, shouts, or gunshots on TV. To wake up and see a flood, war, chaos or earthquake in a movie and think it's real (hey, that pretty much sounds like the real news) can be a scary thing. It can be like a Clint Eastwood movie: Good, Bad, and Ugly!

Instead of the television blaring throughout the day, make sure there are books, magazines and music to calm, soothe, and entertain. Play the music while you talk about making some changes in the space and play some while you're working on the changes. While the music is playing the job is less demanding and can be worked on in the smooth rhythm of your, and your loved ones' choice. You'd be surprised how fast the work goes when music is leading the way. My father recently painted for hours while listening to the Temptation's *"For Lovers Only."*

11 Lighten Up!
Turn on the lights, turn up the wattage.

There isn't a day or night that goes by that I'm not squinting and trying to read in the dark or in a room so dimly lit that it may as well be totally dark. Each time I do it I think the same thing: my vision is getting horrible. I might try to read a recipe in the kitchen without turning on the lights (big mistake) or I'll attempt to read tiny newspaper or magazine print without turning on the lights. Whenever I do this, I find myself squinting, getting very annoyed and concerned that my eyes are changing to the bad side. Then, I have the bright idea to turn on a light, well, usually it's my husband's bright idea! Amazing. Instantly repaired vision.

Always put some light on the subject — the more the better. From age 50 on, the eyes require that lights have more wattage and light intensity in order to attain a comfortable level for reading and seeing. Lights that add brightness, and don't underestimate this, make the words more legible and encourage us to read and write also cuts down on our agitation.

At any age and in any condition, we all have night habits. To make certain all are safe while taking care of whatever those habits are, we need to be able to hear clearly and to see clearly to create security. Don't ask the people you're caring for if they want more light because they'll probably tell you not to bother, or not to worry, which are all, by the way, key words that translate to "Yes, of course, why do you have to ask?" Don't ask, just add more light for them. There's no way around an electric bill that's too high. For me, no matter what I do there's never a drop in the electric charges. My husband and I vacationed for three weeks last year and the electric bill went up. Go figure.

I read a great article about studies being done with light for older eyes and the need for more wattage in order to see more clearly and comfortably. Eyes that have more light around them might not be so bad after all. In the kitchen under the counters so recipes can be read, in the bathroom so a person can see what they're doing and to what, in the hallway and by the steps to help eliminate falls (which are a leading cause of injury related death for the elderly), in the bedroom for recreation, for reading prescriptions, and matching colors when getting dressed—add more light.

Light is necessary for body rhythm. Lights on: wake up, lights off: time to rest. If the body doesn't get enough light it gets confused. Lack of light may even cause depression. It's been documented that there is a high occurrence of depression induced by lack of light in a lot of nursing homes and is probably on the rise in hospitals where patients are left alone all day in dark or dimly lit rooms. Usually, people in these facilities who are not concerned with the health of the patient resort to encouraging sleep so the people they're caring for will require less care and attention. If you're visiting and caring for someone who's in a hospital or care facility of some kind, make sure you speak to the doctors and nurses in charge so that your loved one isn't living in the dark or kept in the dark to encourage them to sleep more. Demand that the lights are turned on and that the wattage is increased in private rooms and in common areas and remember to check and insist that eyeglasses are always close at hand for your loved one.

Wherever you're giving care, make sure that the curtains are opened during the day and that lights are turned on and up during the day and at night when they're needed. Ease the strain and put some light on the subject

#12 Use those Catalogs (and Take a Good Look At Goodwill)

Find what you need and what you didn't know you needed. By now, I'm sure it's clear that you are going to need many things you didn't know you needed and things you didn't even know existed. After one or two surgeries for you, a loved one, a friend or relative of a friend, you'll be properly introduced to gadgets for reaching, picking up, magnifying, massaging, squeezing, resisting, and rolling around. There are also the pillboxes, telephone amplifiers, rubber disks for opening bottles and jars, and slippers to warm and cushion the feet. Those odd job-like places, dollar stores, and the Goodwill are great for stocking up on items you didn't know you wanted or needed. As long as you check the date on a food product and you're not worried about the strength or weight-bearing safety of the product (for example, don't buy cheap chairs or cheap walking canes) shopping for less will really help your wallet. Shirts, blouses, day dresses, night clothes, T-shirts, sheets, pillow cases, games and gadgets galore can be had for the price they should be—if you look around. Don't forget to ask the people at work because it's possible some of your coworkers have the very items that would serve you and your loved one just fine.

If you're like me, and I'm certainly like most people I know, you're always looking for a bargain. Find what you need at half the price, find what you didn't know you needed cheap, cheaper or free.

#13 Get Ready, Get Set & Stay Organized
Just be sure to keep an eraser handy.

We have entered, or been thrust into, the age of useful technological equipment. There are Blackberries, iPhones, Notebooks, Palm Pilot's, cell phones (that even sounds antiquated, now), beepers, e-mail, faxes, phones (yep, still plain old land-line phones) and computers for your desks and laps. Pick one, just one, you can use to schedule and note all the caregiving duties and appointments you have regarding your loved one and make it accessible for anyone else. I suggest the use of a good old-fashioned calendar with enough space on it to write notes. Keep the calendar in your kitchen, a good common area for notes so that everyone can see it and know what can and needs to be done on a daily basis whether you're there or not to offer reminders. Whether your relatives or the ones you care for are independent or require assistance for inside or outside activities, everyone should be kept apprised of the daily routines.

These days you don't have to get just any calendar. You can take the time to pick one you really like and can relate to in some large or small way. The selection for calendars is astounding. Like mountains? They've got plenty. Are you an animal lover? Calendars with those photos are there, too. National parks, motorcycles, celebrities, cars, rivers and streams float your boat? They're all out there. Find one and use it to stay organized. The days and months are right there in clear view with writing space to use and see at a glance for you and yours and all concerned.

Planning is good business, a time saver and generally, a money saver. Plan your menus and schedule your time but be open to change. Plan where to and when to shop for groceries. I'm a list maker and sometime list breaker. When I follow the list I save time and money. When I'm out and the list is kicked-back hiding at home, I lose time and money, duplicate items and can't remember what's on sale or where.

Buy what other people like, not just you, and you won't waste money. When you plan and remember to buy what people like, your time isn't spent tossing out what no one eats. I spoke to a caregiver who likes, no loves, mayonnaise. She told me recently that she only buys the best food for her uncle but she still can't get him to eat. She said she buys Best Foods mayo because she herself likes it, and Jif peanut butter, because again, she herself likes it. I told her when it's for her uncle buy what he likes, period, which was actually Miracle Whip salad dressing and not mayonnaise at all. He also preferred a brand of peanut butter I don't even remember. Buy what people like.

When possible, make shopping together an outing. Split up if you can while you're out and give each other some space to make individual selections and new selections. Try going to outdoor markets for a nice trip away and to pick out fruit and vegetables or baked goods. Take the time, sometimes, to be extravagant. We know that honey shouldn't cost $12.00 anywhere, but at a feel-good shopping outing, buy it. Who knows, it may be worth the price in one way or another.

Plan your menus but be flexible enough to allow for meal changes so that when people are helping you out by doing the cooking and bringing meals for you, you can make a change without big problems. Plan for a week, shop for a week and cook something that will give you a few meals, not just one. One large chicken will give you a chicken dinner, a couple of chicken sandwiches, broth and small pieces of chicken that are great for cooking white beans, and if you really know how to clean the bones, you'll be able to make gravy and have that over rice or baked potatoes. I know you've got some great ideas to put in place, just remember to use them.

The woman who cared for my mother-in-law was notorious for scheduling. She had a schedule for indoor and outdoor activities, schedules for cleaning, scheduling for relaxing, scheduling for fun time. Scheduling is still the best timesaver and lists work well, too. And since this is called real life, keep an eraser handy.

I have to squeeze this in here for you because it falls somewhere between all the new gadgets I mentioned earlier and knowing what's going on in your days. In order for your loved one to reach you, pick one, just one, device that you prefer to be contacted on. Give one number that you will check regularly during the day, every day, and give that number to those you care for in order for them to be able to reach you immediately. That way, no one gets frantic trying to locate one of the five different numbers to reach you and you won't go just as nuts trying to retrieve messages or take calls from more than one source.

Older people and anyone who lives with you and are under your care, or a person who needs to contact you about your loved ones, will all appreciate you streamlining their efforts. This will also work well for doctors and their offices because they will generally not call four or five numbers to get in touch with one person.

Having one number will eliminate some stress and just makes good common sense.

> **Hint: Make it easy for everyone — near or far — to keep in touch.**

Chapter IV

I AM

#14 Play the Music to Entertain
Good music makes everybody want to move.

Good music can make a moment better. I listen to most anything that has a beat that blends cultures or is rife with lyrics that suit me in my moment, but everyone's not that forgiving to my moments. Playing music you love is what will entertain you. Music your loved one loves is what will entertain them.

Recently, I had to stock my mother's room with what she liked and what she needed to have close at hand after hip surgery. So that I could have a stack of the music that entertained her, I asked her to refresh my memory on some of the songs she used to play during parties and some of the ones she still puts on the CD player. She mentioned Marvin Gaye, which immediately brought a smile to her face and to my mind came the image of Marvin (listen to me, calling him Marvin like I knew him) in his knit cap singing to no one but my mother. I also had the memory of my mother and father moving around the room like they could dance forever even with my fathers' two left feet! Lou Rawls and everything he ever sang was next on her list, followed by The BeeGees, Kenny Rogers and Dinah Washington. Then came the incomparable Nat King Cole, the smooth saxophone of Kenny G, and the energy of Gerald Levert. She added The Temptations, Nancy Wilson, Aretha Franklin, for both her gospel and secular songs, and Gladys Knight rounded out the list. She could have gone on longer but I stopped her.

I thought while listening to Mom, that I hadn't heard this music playing in or around her space. It was time to turn it all around. I collected the music played it, and watched my mom move, read, bob her head, exercise, and recover to the music she loves.

Be determined to pipe music back into the home and into the space of your loved one. I'm all for gospel music and I understand some people don't even want secular music in their homes, but for your loved one, make sure it isn't all about meeting the maker. Spice it up a little for pure entertainment, whether it's gospel music or secular music, turn it up and pump it up with talk about better tomorrows.

Just play the beats and lyrics that have always brought a smile to your face and to theirs. Take some of the old and mix in some new rhythms that might make you and the person you're caring for feel younger and more alive. Entertain yourself and your loved one with music that makes you feel good, makes them feel good and makes everyone want to get up and move and use their bodies. I've got to go to Bob Marley again and tell you to "...forget your sickness and dance..."

#15 Feed the Spirit Don't Smother it
I'm talking about your spirit and theirs.

Think of one of your good daydreams or fantasies about looking good, feeling good, and ruling the world or maybe just win-
ning one argument at home. That's the spirit talking.

Inside each of us, I believe there's a spirit that makes us feel
younger, stronger, smarter, more beautiful and sexier. I'm talking
about the spirit that makes us vital, makes us feel alive and gives
us the drive and determination we need to keep going. And
when we're stressed, tired, or sick, I think this same spirit gets
weak and run down and stops thinking forward and stops being
creative. The spirit, if left undernourished, sort of just gives up.
When that happens, we get lackluster and complacent, listless
and careless.

As a caregiver, I'm sure that stress and fatigue have booted
your spirit out and that it has probably hit pay dirt by now. Now
magnify the feeling of stress and fatigue you feel with the reality
of loss and losing control, poorer health, and loss of a home and
maybe strength and youth. Add taking orders, changing plans,
hearing about and having more surgery and the spirit gets
crushed. Apply that to your loved one and you'll get a sense of
how their spirit must be gasping for breath. Whatever the circumstances and current state of health for them, their spirit
probably hit the dirt long ago. Get back the spirit.

Take a moment to feel bad, real bad it's okay and then move forward. Find out what the spirit is inside for you and for your loved
one, then feed them and keep the spirits alive.

On an episode of an HGTV. program, a man who'd recently moved into a house found photos and memorabilia of the former owner shortly after he started renovating. He had known the woman who'd lived there but said he never knew her as the person he saw in the photos or had started to read about in the letters he'd uncovered in the house. While cleaning out one of the rooms, he discovered a box of hats. He said they were beautifully crafted and very classy and not at all like the woman he remembered who had lived in the house. He said what he saw in photos was a more exciting and more fascinating woman than the one he'd known. What I think he saw in the photos was the woman when her spirit was more alive.

Hint: What's needed can also be what's wanted.

It's easy for us to see when the spirit of another person is absent and it's probably when the person seems out of sorts. Until we walk in the proverbial shoes of anyone else, we don't really understand what they've been through that brought them to where they are or where they feel they're going.

A young woman in her mid-twenties once agreed to have a complete makeover for the Oprah show. This wasn't a makeover about the popular new looks for the sake of ooohs and aaahs kind of transformation. This particular young woman agreed to be transformed into a woman in her late 70's. The best makeup artists were utilized for the project and were able to use computer-generated characteristics that blended the physical traits from her mother and grandmother for more realistic features that enabled them to age her convincingly. So much so, she believed what she saw in the mirror. The artists added padded weight, which slowed her down, and contacts designed to disrupt her good vision. As agreed for the experiment, she also had to live alone in a new home and in a different community populated with people in their 70's and 80's. Her only contacts would be people she'd meet at a nearby senior citizens' home.

Through the fear and loneliness of being in a new environment, having joint pain brought on by the additional weight of the padding, and the sadness of having none of her friends or family around, she learned. Through the disadvantage of being treated like an older person with frailties rather than the young, strong attractive person she really was, she learned more about the person inside herself and some of the what our elders endure daily.

She quickly learned what none of us knows until we find ourselves in similar situations and get to feel it first hand. Illness or being incapacitated and feeling wrecked, weakened, worn-out and useless in unfamiliar territory manages to take all the power a person feels inside and breaks it. It breaks their spirit.

In order to find and feed the spirit, you have to be truthful. We all do. Know yourself and the people you're caring for — be honest about the struggles, changes, challenges, likes and dislikes for each of you. You have to consider what you're going through and what those you're caring for have gone through and are still going through. Get to the good stuff in life any way you can. Don't worry about making or taking gigantic strides because little steps work wonders to feed the spirit.

For yourself, find time to free your spirit. Wear the hat you like that makes or made you feel young or sexy and don't be afraid to break the brim, you know, pull it to the front and push it off to the side. Wear cologne, or wear beautiful and oh so stylish (super sharp) shoes and then reach deep inside to find some of what and who you used to be and be some of that vivacious, handsome, debonair, daring, happy person again. Put on the pants that hug your body. Play catch or table tennis. Hold in your stomach and strut your stuff.

Don't give it a lot of thought. Lighten and feed your spirit and help your loved one feed theirs. You'll both feel better about life.

#16 People Need Purpose
Chores and hobbies are good for the soul.

This tip is no different than any of the others in that it's up to you to determine what your particular circumstances are. You have to decide what works for you and yours or make adjustments so that you can incorporate these good ideas to help make your life easier, fuller, and better. And so it is with people needing purpose. As long as we're talking about a living, breathing, person with the hopes of a future or needing the hope to better see their future, purpose is important for human beings. Purpose makes one feel needed, necessary, and worthy, and may well keep our lights shining brighter.

I've seen caregivers overlook the value of purpose and see it as a burden for those they're giving care to or presume that allowing a person (or encouraging a person) to do nothing except rest or not move a muscle might be the best thing for them. It isn't. What it does is have a reverse effect and encourages people to exist without a reason. It puts more of a burden on the caregiver and leaves the loved one bored and totally dependent with too much time to think about nothing but themselves.

Helping people find purpose or keep purpose in their lives is easier to do than we might think, so there's no reason to make it difficult. Keep it simple and you'll accomplish a world of good. From sharing knowledge to sharing chores that are appropriate for their particular situation, to making time for hobbies, your loved one will find that they haven't outlived their usefulness. They'll feel they are contributing in some way to their upkeep and are needed to enrich the time and days of others. Find out what will add substance to the daily life of the person you're caring for and help them get involved at a level that is satisfactory. Chores and responsibilities can be anything from sorting and folding clothes to washing dishes, taking care of correspondence, making telephone calls, mending clothes, knitting items for sale and gifts, caring for plants and scheduling home maintenance. So much, but notice, I didn't mention babysitting. Give it some thought and talk about it and find ways for everyone to get involved and stay involved in day-to-day living. Once you learn to curtail the use of these three words: "I'll do it" well, four actually, you'll be on your way to making days better for you and yours.

The importance of hobbies as part of one's purpose should never be left on the sideline of life because hobbies keep the juices flowing, something I think is necessary to keeping people whole. If you have hobbies you enjoy, make sure you're still involved with them. Find new space to continue your projects if you have to, scale back if you need to, but for your sanity, keep your hobbies alive. Find out from your loved one which hobbies they like, have pursued in the past and can still work on, or make suggestions for new ones they can get started on now. If there is a group or activity center where they can get involved outside the home it would be even better. Do some research and encourage the people you care for to do the same. Whether it's through painting, sketching, sculpturing, singing, writing music, window gardening, ceramics, reading, writing, or volunteering time, help your loved one find a way to use their talents and energy so they feel they have more purpose. You'll find you're both able to have some mental and physical loads eased.

Common sense tip:
Don't waste the mind, the body, or the hands!

Fear might be one of the strongest emotions for all of us and has got to be an even stronger emotion for people who have lost some of their strength and control. Caregivers often have questions on how to break through the fear their loved ones harbor. When I speak to groups of those being cared for, they express fear about being alone, fear about having lost control, fear about not being strong, and about not feeling useful or not having purpose. I suggest to the caregivers and to those being cared for that being on common ground, doing familiar tasks, and regaining some control of a situation helps to ease fear. I tell them to try cooking.

One of the quickest and best ways to help people keep or regain their purpose is to suggest and encourage involvement in the kitchen. Never underestimate the power of peeling or mashing (yes, physically mashing) potatoes, making turkey meatloaf, or just cleaning out the refrigerator or freezer. Kitchen work can be like therapy 101. Its own kind of course, but therapy just the same. I think cooking and serving 'cooked love' is a purposeful task indeed. Your loved one can spend some time in the kitchen with or without you to prepare old or new favorites, ground themselves, and feel like they have purpose again. Make sure while all the cooking or cleaning is going on in the kitchen, that you take the time to listen to and share stories about past cooking episodes of other relatives and let your loved one share their kitchen trials and tribulations!

I remember a story from my Gram about one of the times she visited my mom and sat in the kitchen with her while mom got dinner ready. She told me that mom had a beautiful roast that she'd carefully seasoned the same way she herself had always done, and then cut off one of the ends of the roast, the way she herself had always done, and then tossed the cut piece of meat in the garbage. What? Wait, Gram had never done that. She asked mom why in the world she was throwing away a good piece of meat? Mom told her she had always seen her do it and thought the ends weren't good to eat. My Gram told me that the reason she had always cut off the meat was because her pan was too small. And, she said, she never threw the cut part out, but put it in the refrigerator to use later.

Salute the power of chores and hobbies. Dear caregivers, pass on some chores, tell and laugh about the anecdotes, and help keep the hobbies alive!

#17 Good Health Comes in Assorted Flavors
Sometimes you have to cook something that's just good eating!

Try this, beat an egg, burn some bacon, melt some butter, and cook up some love like you really know how to and *want* to cook. This is more on the tip 'therapy' I just talked about. I'll call it therapy 102, kitchen talk, kitchen time, kitchen therapy (and it comes on strong when you mix it with music therapy).

Every day we're all bombarded with news about the high-energy food of the day, the cure-all food of the moment, and the best foods to eat for breakfast, lunch and dinner. You may have also noticed that this oh so well researched list changes regularly.

Remember when (forgive a sentence that starts off like our parents talking—but it's okay, we're parents, too) most of us would wake up to big breakfasts of sausage or bacon and eggs with a couple slices of white toast? Or maybe three pancakes with strips of bacon on the side, or French toast? We may have had large glasses of whole milk and juice and fruit galore. Eggs were most always included, meat was an expected and accepted side, and we seemed to have been doing just fine. Times changed, and I believe most of what has changed that causes problems today is not so much what the food is, but what it isn't. It's hard to find real food. What's on most supermarket shelves is scary and we don't know what's in it or where it's from. Don't worry, this isn't the place for my discussion on the nonsense they put in food and the good they've taken from it that has caused stomach ailments and who knows what else for a huge percentage of the population. Indigestion after a meal that has mystery ingredients, anyone?

Eating used to be fun and cooking was even better.

Kitchens were usually good places to be while you watched your loved ones and good friends prepare their favorites. Cooking and the aromas from cooking made you feel good. Microwaves are great but when you reheat store-bought food for a minute and a half you just can't recreate the smell of thick cod with tomatoes and onions cooking in the oven for a couple of hours, or a chicken roasting for three hours, or pork roasting forever. Unfortunately, like most things that go on in our lives today, all cooking takes a lot of time and real cooking takes longer than that. I know you don't have time to do it everyday, but give it a try to make you feel better. To make the people you care for want to eat and to make your house have the aroma of good living, still living!--cook something real and cook something together that helps bring back memories.

I've got so many stories about food I can hardle believe it. Let me share a couple of them to try and get my point across. I have caregivers I speak to and coach regularly and on occasion I've been asked to coach those for whom they give care. One patient I know, whose caregiver I speak with on a regular basis, always has a request for coffee ice cream or pinto beans. I've known the patient for years and I always think back to when she used to make three flavors of ice cream every summer when we were all growing up. She'd make peach, vanilla, and coffee. When she asks for beans I remember her mother and how she would cook a pot of pinto beans with hatch peppers at least once a month.

The requests and cravings from our loved ones might seem bizarre to us but sometimes it's easy to see why real food might be necessary. Real food and having some of those memories brought back might help to get elders and the people you care for to eat again. We've all got some food memories. You've got some and your loved one has some. Cook something.

What's good about fruitcake? They take a beating about how they're made to last for years, are hard as bricks, and that nobody likes them. Wrong! For some reason, one year my mother started making fruitcakes to give away during the Christmas season, when it was a real season with people taking off work and enjoying it as a holiday. She'd start in late September by soaking the filling for the fruitcake in alcohol. It seems like every week there was another step to getting to the final product of the fruitcake. After a few years of her making the cakes, some people had special requests for more cakes. Some went so far as to request more nuts or more alcohol. My brother liked more alcohol and as Mom's fruitcake was the only one I've ever actually eaten, I'd ask for more raisins. Mom's friends started putting in their orders in August for her cakes. When mom started baking the fruitcakes the house was filled with an indescribable aroma of bitter and sweet. For weeks we smelled fruitcake throughout the house and we loved it. Why am I talking about my mother's fruitcake? Because looking back on it now, I know that it relaxed her, made her feel good, kept me and my sister in the kitchen with her, and it filled our house with the best aromas.

Taking a cake out of a box or cookies from the supermarket out of a bag is a treat to be sure, but that will not fill the corners of the house with warmth. Bake something. This is a sometime therapy course, because nobody has the time they'd like to spend in the kitchen. Most often whatever is prepared in the supermarket will find it's way to our table, aroma accompanying it or not.

Make alterations with the salt and oil if you have to, but set your kitchen burners to "ready to cook!" I do not advocate breaking doctors' strict rules, but I suggest that sick people and the elderly will eat when they're given food they like, food that tastes good and food that smells good to them. I love to share the story about my Gram and whiting.

Most people who are elderly or being cared for might have a difficult time finding something satisfying to eat. It's hard for them to just get up the will, the determination, or the interest in eating. Some of that might have to do with the fact that a lot of the foods that have been enjoyed in the past don't taste the same. You also need to understand that many foods don't have the same flavor to an older, medicated palate and that many of the favorite foods have been taken from the healthy list. Though for many of those over 100 I've heard comments that all food in moderation is what keeps them going. That doesn't work for everybody, but it works for a lot of people. Real food though, not the make-believe food we eat too often: yellow tubs of what we can't believe, cream that requires no refrigeration, precooked bacon, fruit and vegetables out of their season, colossal chickens, and endless shrimp? How? Really, what are we thinking?

Anyway, back to my grandmother and the fish. She loved whiting, and unfortunately, she loved it fried. After about a week of her not eating much of anything, I asked her if she would eat a whiting sandwich if I fixed one for her. A bright smile came across her face immediately. One reason for it's brightness was because she wanted the fish, and two, she knew I couldn't cook it.

I'd hit a chord and a good one to be sure. I went straight to my aunt and told her I was going to the restaurant down the street to get whiting for Gram to have for dinner. My aunt said I'd better not give it to Gram. She thought the bones in the fish might cause a problem and that Gram didn't need anything fried. I said, Gram has enough sense to take the bones out of her mouth and as far as the fried part, eating two pieces of fried fish will be better for her than not eating anything at all. I got the fish and sat with my Gram while she bit down carefully on each piece to make sure she got out any leftover bones. I put on the stereo and played Caribbean Queen and was in total joy at the sight of her eating something she enjoyed with great background music.

The point here is not to disobey any doctors' orders, but to realize that eating a little of one food is better than eating nothing of a lot of them. Call the primary care physician for the person you care for if you're extremely concerned or if their condition is such that even a bit of certain foods might cause serious interactions or health problems. I do not suggest putting anyone at risk but I do encourage using common sense and finding a happy medium. Remember to bring in assorted flavors and a variety of foods and remember what your loved ones really like. Peach ice cream, ginger ale, fried chicken, broiled fish, spaghetti, meatloaf, or lasagna. Whatever it is, put it on the menu and make it available. If you have to, alter when necessary with skim or 1% milk, light ice cream, oven fried and skinless chicken, no sodium sodas, turkey meatloaf and part skim and low fat cheeses. Then do yourself a favor and use those oh so handy disposable pans, and then, hear me loud and clear, dispose of them.

You can do it, dear caregivers. Find a way and do it. In a world where food is the center of so many social activities and holidays, cooking good food will bring more satisfaction and nutrition than you think. Maybe you can even take a walk for exercise after the meal and spark a renewed spirit at the same time.

Hint: Write down shared recipes and share them.

#18 People Don't Change, Situations Do
Help your people find 'like-people.'

Be A People Person

Here's something we boomers are darn good at: marketing, self promoting and networking. Use your networking skills. I know that even the most introverted of you have had to put forth an effort in your caregiving role to meet and greet new people like never before, now use those skills to help your people find people like them. Surround your loved one with people of like spirit— their spirit my friend, not yours, and make sure it's a good spirit.

Whether it's in your home that you're giving care, in a facility, in a hospital, or in their home, help your loved ones find people they like who have similar interests or backgrounds or philosophies. People who are like them. Now is not the time to try to change your elders. They like what they like and whom they like. Let me reiterate because when you remember this it's easier on all concerned: They like what they like and whom they like. People don't change, situations do. If they're independent, insecure, nervous, or demanding, they'll be the same except with more of the strongest traits showing, because I sense that when we're down and out, the strongest part of ourselves surfaces.

If your loved one takes pleasure in debating current events, painting outdoors, walking in the park, playing bridge or bid whist, visiting museums or concert halls, help them find like people who enjoy those pastimes, too.

Finding like people for your people might even encourage more of a wellness attitude for them. Perhaps there'll be less dependency for each of you and more excitement from the people you care for because, let's face it, they require more stimulation than you can provide if you try to be their only social reference system. Finding like people for your loved one might also bolster their confidence so they want to get up, get dressed, and converse more.

If you're really stumped about finding people of like spirit for your loved one, do some research to find out about local activities and who's doing what and where they're doing it. Watch the community bulletin channels that are on most cable systems and read the activities (dances, bus tours, day trips, etc.) listed for seniors. Start by looking for a facility that offers classes or trips for elders who are in similar situations as your loved ones. Ask questions when you call the center about all programs and opportunities for the participants to interact, and who attends, because after all, this is about people of like spirits getting together.

Think about activities outside the medical arena; think beauty salons, churches, barbershops, museums, and restaurants. The people who frequent these places will provide a huge network system to work with, either filled with people you can get together with the person you care for or filled with people who can give you leads. You, in essence, will be a matchmaker of sorts and will find out where those people are. Find like people and your loved one will flourish in many ways.

It may well be easier on you to drive a couple of elders to a location where they can spend time together rather than for you to spend your time participating in activities you don't enjoy or with someone who might need to socialize with new people. Think of it as break for you, and a chance for being with like people for the person you care for.

Make this work in your house, in their house, in a hospital, or in an assisted living home. Help people find like people, people like them who will bring light, smiles, and commonality to their lives.

Hint: There's nothing better than talking-it-up
with people who 'get you'.

Chapter V

GET BACK TO BASICS

#19 Cleanliness Can Still Be Had With Soap and Water
It's not rocket science, keep it clean and most
germs won't know what to do.

Basically, it makes good sense. There's water, water everywhere and it still has hundreds of uses. Water is used for cooking, drinking, for cold packs and hot packs, cleaning, bathing, and easing and soothing away stress, and tension. It also attacks dirt. With the advent of those little bottles of sanitizing gels, we've forgotten all about the usefulness of water. We all pay good money through our taxes to have access to clean water in this great country of ours, and now it seems we're afraid to use it. Use it you should, just like we all used to do, for the basics like keeping things clean. From our hands to countertops, it's not rocket science, keep it clean and a lot of germs won't know what to do.

I know you've seen people in public bathrooms passing right by the sink and taking out their bottle of sanitizing gel. I once overheard a person whom I presumed to have been the mother speaking with her young son who was in the bathroom stall with her. As kids will do, this one exclaimed out loud about how big his 'boo' was that he'd just put in the toilet. I was at the sink when the woman came out with the little boy and he told her he had to wash his dirty hands before he left the bathroom. The mother said, no honey, that's what this is for as she took out and held up her little bottle of sanitizing gel. It took all I had to keep quiet and not tell her about the real benefits of using warm water and soap, or that by the time those dirty little fingers were all over the outside of that bottle it was too late. Sure, the sanitizing gel is good in a pinch, but using it in place of soap and water is out of control like cell phone use, which came with the creed that they should only be used in emergencies.

I've heard that washing the hands and body with soap and warm water is still the best defense against fighting germs and helps keep the skin's immunity strong to be able to fight infection. If warm soap and water doesn't work for your situation or your care requires you to wear gloves for your safety and the health of the person you're caring for, do what you have to do. If it's gloves you have to use, make sure you use them appropriately. Don't misuse them like some people I see in food preparation and serving areas in restaurants and fast food chains or in hospitals with people who believe they can collect money, clean floors, scratch their heads, fix their hair, cough into the gloves, and then prepare food or be sanitary with the same gloves on. Where are the health inspectors when you need them?

I think the marketing mavens have done too good a job of filling us with fear about germs and using the fear to sell us junk we can do without. Sure, there are some timesaving cleaners out there, but I think it makes good common sense to stick with what you need. Maybe adding a little vinegar or bleach to hot water will boost your cleaning power and disinfect just fine but I get crazy when I see television commercials where people use bleach to wipe crumbs off countertops or ketchup off refrigerator handles. Hot soapy water or damp paper towels will do just fine most times. What we need to remember is that warm to hot water and soap has to be used for it to work! Use the other stuff that you can rub on your hands to sanitize them if you want, but please people, use hot water and soap as often as possible to wash your hands followed with clean towels or paper towels. Use soap and water to clean hands, bodies, chairs, benches, and countertops. Remember how often we used to see soap and water used for clean up?

Can you think back to when we used to see the hospital staff in the patients' rooms using hot water and soap or disinfectant to clean floors, bed rails, chairs, and window seats? Remember when nurses used to clean the patients with warm water and soap? Remember they wore less jewelry because the general consensus was that jewelry would catch and hold dirt and germs? Remember when doctors and nurses used hot water, soap, and a brush to scrub their hands, nails, and arms clean? Am I the only one who thinks that when doctors and other hospital workers used hot water and soap that there were probably fewer cases of hospital related infections?

If you're cleaning up bodily fluids or solids, you might need or want stronger ammunition bolstered by the scent of pine and disinfectant spray, but for regular cleaning and on a regular basis, please try using soap and very warm to hot water.

I believe water also restores. I know patients who've said the best feeling they had was when they were able to take a full water bath or shower — not a bottled sanitizing gel clean-up. Warm water and soap on a full thick wash cloth, and a soft towel to dry off afterward is another way to spell relief. Find a way to include bathing or water soaking for the person you care for. If tubs and showers aren't an option for you, study your budget and call on some friends who are in the business of redesigning, do some research and/or get creative.

Taking showers doesn't necessarily mean standing up. You only need to get the person beneath the water for them to shower. There are plastic chairs and benches you can put inside a tub and they're lightweight and durable. If you really can't get your loved one to the shower or tub, find a way to get the water to them. Those large outdoor pools have got to be good for something other than smashing the grass. Find a way to let the water rain down so the body can be soothed and cleansed. This is of course, keeping in mind the doctor's orders and/or if you're concerned about areas of the body which aren't supposed to get wet. It's getting the person to the water that's important. Those walk-in tubs that are advertised look ideal, but if the only way you'll be able to get one installed is by hitting the lotto, consider some other options that will provide comfort and still allow you to make use of water for bathing. This creative bathing is another reason for extra bathing suits and T-shirts from super discount stores. They come in handy so stock up for more reasons than one.

Common Sense Tip: Scent it Up!

After all the bodies, floors, doors, etc. are fresh and clean, don't overlook adding scents to your space and the space of your loved one. These days, scents and sounds are used to lure customers into stores and to encourage them to shop in supermarkets and department stores. They're great at home, too.

It's been proven that what you hear and smell while you're

shopping affects your mood and makes a difference to your shopping experience and, possibly, whether or not you'll make a purchase. Music usually puts me in a much better mood while I'm in the supermarket. I like to breeze through the isles humming or singing along to the old and new songs that are piped in, but it doesn't encourage me to buy more. My pocketbook and shopping list dictate what will come home with me. Either way, I appreciate the music because I feel better and move through faster when the tunes are playing.

Using aromatherapy and scents from oils found in nature is said to cure, calm and set a particular frame of mind. I don't necessarily subscribe to the beliefs that scents alone can cure ailments or ward off negative associations, but I don't downplay the benefits of soothing, relaxing and freshening aromas filling our spaces. To refresh the house and stimulate the olfactory senses, good smells are perfect. Since most fragrances permeate different areas of a home or might be potent in small areas, make certain you aren't offending anyone. I love scents, those being the scents and fragrances I love, which is to say, not all of them. I keep sage and white grass Smudge sticks on my nightstand and usually have lavender scented candles in the bath.

All the rooms in my house have different personalities so I use different fragrances in each one. I encourage caregivers to try different aromas for different moods for themselves and their loved ones. From floral potpourri to simmering pots and fragrant candles that smell good even unlit (which is much safer for many people) lemon, basil, bergamot, sweet orange, peppermint, eucalyptus, tangerine, sweet grass, juniper, lavender, sage, and cedar wood, all are wonderful scents. Some like to use scented oil for the skin but I've heard that some are too strong to put directly on the body.

There are scents that are supposed to evoke emotions (check the magazine ads and perfume counters to find out what I mean) or watch a special on how scents are created and the chemistry behind it all to calm and settle or invigorate. If the scent doesn't smell good to you or the person you're caring for, then it doesn't matter what it's supposed to do, it's not the one for you.

Do your research and check with your loved one before putting aromas that you enjoy around everyone else's nose.

#20 Sunshine Heals and Blue Skies Mend
Let daylight be part of your therapy.

Let the house wake up and let the new day begin with sunlight, music, and exercise. Open the curtains and let the sunshine or rainy skies in. Whatever the weather, leave the guilt and problems from the day before and start by bringing the new day inside. Don't let the people you care for live inside with no sunshine coming in, no defining of the old and new days, and no thought of the outside world. Whether they're confined to the bed or able to get up and move around, sunshine and blue skies mend and seeing new days usually gives a person a renewed sense of purpose.

There is an undeniably good feeling in seeing a new day of sunny skies, rain, or snow. Whatever the weather, it's still a new day. Our bodies need it, our minds need it, and we need to keep our internal clocks set with it. Sun is good to help dry out damp homes, kill some forms of mold, and always, to lift spirits. Dark houses seem to me to be like dungeons and you don't want to subject yourself or your loved one to that.

Once you've opened up the curtains and windows, it's a good time to get the body stretched out and moving. Start, end or add to the middle of the day any kind of stretches or movement you can for yourself of course, and for your loved one, too.

I read recently that older people don't like to exercise. I disagree. In the article, they were of course, talking about older people who were put in a room to exercise with folk half their age. I don't want to exercise with people half my age either. Do some physical activities together or encourage your loved one to do some age and condition appropriate things on their own or with a group at a center or club. Some retirement communities, day centers and rehabilitation places have incorporated the use of Nintendo's Wii video game system for exercise and rehab for young and old alike. The players are able to simulate the movement of the actual sports and are said to regain strength and mobility because they're able to focus on the enjoyment of the activity. There's a great television program I refer to caregivers for the elders or loved ones they care for. The half-hour program, "Sit and Be Fit," is designed for movement and stretching from sitting positions or with limited standing. The show includes exercises for the body from fingers to toes, wrists, hands, forearms, buttocks squeezes, leg lifts, leg slides, ankle rotating, foot curls, etc., and feedback told me it was well received. We all do great when we find exercises we enjoy and ones that work for us, from leg lifts to sports to dancing the tango.

Let in the new day and at some point in the day, pipe in and pipe up some music. Then everybody, move those bodies.

#21 Trust Your Instincts: If It Doesn't Look, Sound, or Smell Right...
In the fridge, in the lungs, on those nails.

At some point during your time as a caregiver you'll ask yourself if something is really wrong and whether or not you should call a doctor. Here's where you get to put trust in the instincts you've had all along that have, for some reason, been put on ice while computers and guidelines have done all the thinking for you, me, and the rest of the world. If it doesn't look right, sound right, or smell right to you, it isn't right. Something is wrong.

It's easy to recognize and locate the culprit emitting smelly gases when it's moldy cheese, old chicken, slimy sliced turkey, or milk that got pushed to the back of the refrigerator and soured weeks ago. Bodies give off odors too and signals with color, or lack of, when there are problems brewing.

For a week before I get a cold I can smell the cold festering in my body. I can't describe it, but I know it to be the smell of a cold coming on. My nephew is the only other person I've ever talked to who can smell one coming in his body, too. For about two weeks after a bad cold, in the morning I sound like a cat with a hairball caught in my throat. That's me with and after a cold. But if I see a rash, have a lingering dry or phlegm-filled cough, blood, or seeping pus with the odor of something stale, then I know what's right has gone wrong.

If your loved one has been told to expect some odd occurrences after surgery or as a progression or ending of a particular treatment, then all is running its course. When there's no course to run and something isn't quite right, turn to the lists we've all seen to alert us to when urgent care is needed. They're pretty clear and don't leave a lot of room for confusion. We all know the big ones to look out for: chest pain: call, unexplained bleeding: call: extreme weight loss or weight gain, change in bowel habits, short term loss of vision or movement, slurred speech or loss of memory: get help! You know the full list and the symptoms that demand your attention so don't ignore them, just make certain you learn to distinguish between those symptoms that might signal a problem and those that don't. It will save you and your loved one many headaches.

The person you're caring for might be able to help you make a distinction for some of the normal and abnormal sounds and odd smells of their bodies, too. Ridges on their nails, no color under the nails, purple lips, odd growths anywhere on the body, or a swollen coated tongue are just some of the signals we might get about a problem. Check bodies (yours, too) on a regular basis and know what's what. Let your common sense kick in and investigate what's not normal and find out the cause.

But always, always call a doctor when you're in doubt because instincts can fail us but those EKG's are pretty accurate.

#22 Make Sure There's Good Reason for Any Pills That Are Being Popped
From headaches to a dry cough, check those 'meds'.

Don't let it shock you, but some doctors probably get perks from drug companies to push their pills. This isn't news to anyone who has or has had access to a newspaper or television over the past five years. Drug commercials rule the roost and are pretty much the only commercials we see during the evening news hours when, I suppose, the advertisers presume they have a target market of boomers and elders watching the programs. Literally, we see drugs commercials for pills to treat something from head to toe: for hair growth, more eye tears, less eye tears, the thyroid, depression, high energy, low energy, and on and on it goes. There's a pill to be had for everything. Legs feel restless? You must have restless leg and there's a pill for that. Stomach grumbling sometimes? Must be irritable bowel. There's a pill for that. Cholesterol too high? Blood pressure too low? Worry not, there's a pill for everything. Thank goodness the pills are there when we need them. We are reminded that science is truly wonderful.

But when a host of these pills are going into one body along with other pills to put the patient to sleep, to wake them up, to suppress an appetite, to encourage an appetite, to go to the bathroom, or to stop going to the bathroom, maybe that's too many pills. I've seen patients' cabinets filled with twenty or more pills that have got to, at some point, cause an interaction of more harm than good for the patient. Some major illnesses might call for an arsenal of pills and medications daily, but I'm not talking about those. I'm talking about prescriptions for everything from dry eyes to toe infections. There must be some conditions that can be treated topically with a change in diet, or possibly by not drinking twenty ounces of liquids late at night before bed and then expecting to sleep restfully. I don't think adding another layer of pills that might cause drug interactions is always the answer.

The combination of medications can cause a lot of changes for patients and elders. There are also a number of foods, juices, and other liquids that might cause a negative reaction when they're taken with certain drugs. Check the information that comes with the prescription and ask the doctor about drug interactions and go on line for detailed information about the medication if you feel it's necessary. If you notice changes in the person you're caring for, check the latest medication and notify the doctor if the patient isn't able to (or won't) do it for themselves. Stumbling, loss of sense of taste and smell, headaches, lightheadedness, stomach pain, itching, dry mouth, rashes, swollen tongue, coughing, sneezing, tiredness, depression, and on and on the list can go. Check the prescription because their problem might be attributed to a specific medication, the dosage, and/or a combination of medications.

If it's been determined that a prescription is necessary, have the doctor make sure the dosage is as low as possible for effectiveness. Ask about the safety of the drug for children and elders because, unfortunately, both these demographics are usually ignored during drug trials and they might be at risk for more side effects. Get the answers you need about perscription medication from the doctor or from a nurse.

If you're concerned about the amount of pills prescribed, find out about having them cut back or discontinued. Ask whether or not a particular medication will continue to work as effectively as it did when it was first prescribed. And above all else, inquire as to whether or not the pills can be eliminated if any other life-style change is put in place or certain foods eliminated from the diet.

I know of an 85-year old woman with heart problems who was taking about eighteen pills daily. These drugs were all prescribed at a clinic over a six-month period by multiple resident doctors. Sometime in the seventh month, the woman was released to live in an assisted living home with 24-hour care because she was no longer able to walk or care for herself.

After the woman was settled in her new residence her daughters decided to address the amount of pills she was taking. They thought the pills were actually limiting her quality of life and not designed to make her better but to continue to provide an income for drug companies. The comedian Chris Rock put it best in one of his specials when he said "...the drug companies get you on the comeback..." because you have to keep getting the drugs.

The primary care doctor for the woman was changed from those assigned by the clinic to a private doctor and the patient was taken off three-quarters of her pills, with a promise of banishing more. Now, she can actually walk again and is enjoying life. The new doctor was shocked by the fact that the patient had been treated by so many resident doctors rather than specialists and that many of the prescriptions were causing one to cancel out the benefits of the other.

If you sense a problem find out what's causing it. This won't be easy. Doctors do not particularly want to be questioned about the prescriptions they write or the decisions they make, and may in fact be curt or evasive when questioned. Once, in speaking on behalf of a patient, I had a doctor tell me they would discontinue any and all medication if that's what the patient wanted. He said it was our choice. It was determined that one medication was in fact not needed and another needed to be perscribed in a lower dosage.

Rather than a total hands-off, defensive attitude like I was met with from the doctor, I think physicians should remember they're not above full disclosure or accountability to those for whom they care and the loved ones who speak on behalf of their patients.

The bottom line is, find out what's needed and what's not. Find out what might be causing a problem and get it fixed. If the medication is needed, make sure the patient follows the instructions and that the medication is taken properly. When you get a chance, check out an article from a few years ago that appeared in *AARP* magazine about over-prescribing of drugs in our country and the problems it can cause.

We are all sometimes grasping at straws and hope in a bottle. Make sure there's a reason and a need for the pills being popped.

#23 Don't Go Crazy - Sometimes People Really Can't Get Up or Get Down
Same old floors, older legs.

The thought of another injury will keep the best of us off our feet to avoid accident and on our toes to be careful. There may even come a time when floors will look further away and legs will feel less steady. There might a loss of some strength in the arms and legs and walking on a balance beam will be out of the question. Sick, healing, or even well as can be, sometimes people just can't get up or down so don't call the ambulance just yet.

Try it. Get down, all the way down on the floor. Feeling vulnerable yet? Well, the more "older than 40" you are, the more demanding it is to get up and down and to navigate the best course to get you down and up. Those old football, baseball, skiing, horseback riding, skating, hockey, heck, even bicycle and cheerleading accident injuries catch up. Take that vulnerable feeling brought on by abuse of your own body into consideration when caring for someone else. Sometimes people really can't get off the floor. If you happen to find a loved one on the floor quickly do your own test by asking some detailed questions that might be helpful in ruling out an attack of some kind. Ask their birth date or mention the name of someone they know well and talk about something that happened earlier in the day and ask how they got in the position they're in. Make it conversational and pay attention to all the responses. If all seems to be working well, except of course the weak arms and weak legs, then please, get them up off the floor. If it seems they collapsed or that their brain isn't working properly, get help — 911 — and fast.

If the brain is working okay and the body is just weak and tired keep in mind that there will be a level of embarrassment because being on the floor isn't a dignified place to be unless we get down there and stay down there by choice. It could happen when your loved one is coming out the tub, trying to get off the toilet, you know, in situations where they might not be fully dressed. Be gentle, be respectful (get a robe or towel for them, etc.) and stay calm. If all is well with the brain and health, other than them not eating enough to have strength to get up or they refuse to do exercises for increased strength in the arms and legs, then my boomer friend, help them up. Later on or the next day, stress the exercises that need to be done and find out how to get your loved one started on them immediately. All exercises are good exercises but they can't all be done by everyone. Put the electric can opener away for a while and have available the one that has to be twisted by hand. Add some of the little things back *in* that we all started taking *out* of everyday living--like the can openers or getting up to change the channel--and some strengthening exercises are automatically regained.

If you have to make changes to further personalize the space for comfort and ease of movement, get busy and do it, and always have sturdy bars, walkers or supports of some kind close by. You don't always have to call the ambulance. Find out why they're down there on the floor and get them up!

Chapter VI

TAILOR MADE

#24 The Weight of Words is Heavy — Choose them Carefully
Nothing has more impact than a kind word — except a nasty one!

Get your point across but be gentle with your words.

Once the words are out there there's no getting them back and a bad mouth wreaks havoc on a good spirit. You know what bad words can do to a room, to a house, and to our insides? Think about how horrible you feel after an argument with a loved one. The room may get too warm because you've sent your blood pressure to the roof and you're completely flustered and beside yourself. You may be so angry that you want to run off, slam doors, or break a dish. Instead of ruining your health and everyone else's and before breaking anything you are going to have to replace, take a breath, turn on some good music, and keep your words in check.

> Hint: Put on the first cut of *Dressed To Chill* by Marion Meadows

We all know about the stresses that can cause outbursts, but hopefully, you're taking these tips to heart and are a cooler, calmer dynamo, more aware of what the person you're caring for has gone through or is going through. Not sure what those things might be? Think multiple levels and layers of emotions brought on by pain, frustration, not being able to plan the next day the way they want, fear, loss of power and the loss of control. Keep it all in perspective.

When outbursts come, bad words are spoken and the relationship changes. The love might not change, but the relationship changes. Everyone will get over it (maybe) and apologies will be accepted (maybe!) but nothing will be as it was before. If you have these moments, and we all do, make your apologies immediately then talk it all out honestly soon after. If you can't find a way to talk out your problems with your loved one, talk them out with a professional.

In life, there are always hurts and disappointments for everyone. Let's say you're caring for both your parents. It's possible you always felt your mother didn't love you as much as she loved another sibling, or that your father never understood you. You grew up with this on your mind and now as an adult you're the one giving care to a parent you always thought loved you less. With the thoughts and memories you have, you are already anxious and bitter toward your parents and toward the sibling you felt was loved more. You will probably lash out at your parents to try to make them feel worse than they already do and most likely, you'll lash out at your sibling when you see or speak to them. No matter the circumstances, keep in mind that the people you're caring for love other people, too, whether those people are caring for them or not. You're in the caregiving position you're in either by choice or by default. Save your time and energy and just do what you do, give care, as best you can for the person you love.

It isn't just in the home that caregivers need to pay attention to how their words are spoken, but also out in public: in stores, in doctors' waiting rooms and offices, in the parking lot. Loud or heated discussions about what you the caregiver does, and has done on a daily basis, what other children, friends, or relatives aren't doing, and what illness or mishaps the person you're caring for is dealing with on their own are not healthy topics of conversation. And since there is never a time to 'chastise' your parents or elders to whom you give care, there is no need to tell you that there should be none of that in public or private either.

If you've embarrassed your elders, patients, parents — your parents? — then I'll say it for them, "How could you?!" You're not the boss of them, you embarrass yourself and make you look bad when you yell and scream in public. I've overheard conversations, outbursts, and loud talking from the caregivers that made me cringe and some that made me speak up and offer some tips and suggestions. Caregiver children yelling, threatening, boasting, and insulting their parents or yelling out issues that should be discussed in private (if at all) is a cry for help. Get it. Choose your words carefully because once those bad thoughts take form and turn into ill chosen words, the damage is done and you can't get the words back.

There will be challenges all around but remind yourself that if you're getting angry because you're fighting old battles while trying to tame the new ones, you won't win. I know you've done more than your share, you might be doing more than you want to do, and you've done more than you ever thought you'd have to do. If fatigue and physical and mental strain is causing you to become short tempered and your cargiving duties are piling on more than you can bear, be honest and rethink what might be best for all concerned.

My boomer buddies, try to remember that it's a beautiful world, not a perfect one, and the sun really doesn't rise and set on us and our private worlds. Appreciate the time you have and watch your mouth because the weight of words is really heavy!

> **Common sense tip: you never know who, sick or well, can hear what you say - be careful**

25 Treat Your Loved Ones With Dignity
Build new fences with old-fashioned manners.

When you're inside or out with your loved one, be respectful. If the people you're caring for aren't able to fix their shirt if it needs to be tucked in or buttoned, do it for them. If they are able to and overlook it, suggest to them they do it. Cover up exposed legs and thighs, stomachs, breasts, and chests; comb and brush their hair if they're unable to do it for themselves, and encourage them to do it if they are able. No need to shout to bring attention to the fact that you had to help them bathe or eat that morning or that they got food on their clothes again. You don't make yourself look better by trying to make someone else look bad. People (who all have so much going on in their own lives) generally don't care that you're the only sibling who is doing all the work and don't want to hear about it. Badgering your loved one for past mistakes? Re-read Chapter I. Maybe you should reconsider caregiving. This isn't your chance to get back at anyone for the past but it can be a chance for good change.

It's hard on your loved ones, too. It might sound like a joke to you to talk in front of others about the bathroom habits of the people for whom you give care or any personal 'stuff' you wouldn't want someone talking about if you were the object of the discussion. Think about having another person undress you, clean you or feed you. Or how about having your belongings stored or tossed around because you've lost your home and have to live with new space restrictions in a new home, or you've gotten older and need a little extra help getting around.

Find a support group, find a caregivers' coach (yes, I'm available) then step back and look at the big picture. Don't let work pile up or get out of control. Ask for help and then accept it when it's offered. Most of your friends and relatives know that you're now in the role of caregiver but the whole world doesn't need to know. Don't be rude, bossy, or undignified simply because you're giving care, and under no circumstances should you allow others to be rude or disrespectful or to talk down to anyone who is in your care.

Why some caregivers presume that it's perfectly fine to allow strangers to clean or manage the personal hygiene responsibilities of those they care for, I'll never know. "Needing care" is not synonymous with "can be cared for by any or everyone in the house or who's visiting." If your loved one is incontinent, you might need to have professional help when you're not there or the help of another relative who is approved by your loved one. Don't ask or have casual friends or extended relatives to perform intimate tasks. And if there's anyone you suspect (or your loved one has told you about) of improprieties, sexual advances, inappropriate touching, lewd language, theft of personal items, or abuse of any kind, keep them away from your loved one. You're caring for a whole person so treat them with dignity and you my boomer friends, will be most dignified.

> Hint: Help your loved ones strive for independence
> not total dependency and everybody wins

#26 Be Kind - There's a Fragile, Sensitive Nature In All of Us
Oh, the vanity of woman, the vanity of men.

It's hard to have to use a bedpan or a portable toilet and I think diapers are for babies!

I know one of the definitions for diapers is simply that it is: "a fabric with a distinctive pattern..." but it is also "...a basic garment for infants..." Underpants, not diapers, are recognized as wear for adults and two of the brands I know by name, not recommending, are Poise and Depends. Don't call them diapers when they're for adults because it immediately suggests and signifies that it's an infant, not an adult, who's receiving the care. There is a fragile nature in us all.

The sensitive and private nature of each person is deep inside us and I don't think it vanishes because a person needs care. It probably becomes a continuous slap in the face of our loved ones if they have to submit themselves to personal care from another person, whether it's a loved one or not. None of us wants our muck exposed, our bodies casually handled, or our private parts washed by someone else. It's traumatic for the patient and if this type of care is part of your routine, it's tough on the caregiver who would rather not have to 'see' it all or do it all. It doesn't matter whether it's female to female or male to male or any combination thereof. A woman caring for a woman is hard on both the caregiver and the patient. A woman caring for a man, maybe her father, grandfather, or husband is hard on both. When a man cares for another man or a man has to care for a woman, either his wife or his Mother, it is hard on all concerned.

Some have wrongly called it role reversal when children care for parents and speak about it as though there should be some pragmatic approach. Well, the rolls don't reverse, the situations change. And when the situations change, caregivers have to be very gentle with the fragile nature in those they care for. Caregiving is tough and being cared for is even tougher!

Find a way to manage the personal aspects of caregiving in a dignified way and a way that suits those who need care. Both men and woman are vain and most are used to their privacy and deserve to have respect shown to them and for their situation.

Think about indoor privacy issues. Maybe you can use screens rather than have a portable toilet in the open. Be careful not to walk in unannounced and always speak respectfully to adults about their bodies; breasts and penises are not topics of conversation for caregiving children.

Adults need to be treated like adults not as though they were children. Respect a woman as a woman and a man as a man. Don't talk about wrinkles, drooping boobs, loose skin, or bald spots. Take into account suggestions and requests your loved ones have about their personal wants and implement whichever of those you can. Also, always be mindful of tasks your loved ones can manage for themselves and give them the support, be their cheering squad so to speak, to make sure those tasks are managed by them to boost their sense of independence and yours.

I have a relatively young, male cousin who had a major stroke a little over a year ago. Since I've always known him to be a person who likes to be outside moving around and 'pop calling.' I asked if he was getting out enough. He said his wife who, since his stroke, had to quit her job to care for him, wants him to sit in the backyard in his robe and he refuses to do that. He said he doesn't want his neighbors to see him sitting out there just looking at the sky. I suggested to him that he let his wife know that he's ready and capable to do more on his own and would prefer walking at the track with a friend until he can build up strength.

Don't presume you know what the other person is thinking if they aren't able to speak for themselves. Even if you've lived together for years, minds can't be read. In the comic strip For Better of For Worse by Lynn Johnson which appears in most daily newspapers, there's been the ongoing challenge of the father being rehabilitated after a having stroke. His wife who is also his caregiver is overburdened, sad, and exhausted. She also thinks she knows how to interpret every sound that comes out of his mouth. She doesn't, and through the magic of the strip, we get to see what the patient is really saying when the wife is sure it's something else.

You'll also be respectful of the fragile nature when you know *when* to discuss *what*. Don't choose meal times to vent about your caregiving duties, to complain, or be insistent. Have meal times reserved for time to eat together in peace with lighthearted spirits and the time to have good conversations. Don't talk at night or late in the evening about the worst parts of life or about all the challenging issues facing you and the world. Set aside times for discussions about lifes' aggravations, business and financial issues and the future. And then, stick with those times.

You, dear caregiver, are easily agitated these days and you know that your loved one and the people you care for at their wit's end, too. Not healing as quickly as they'd like, or not healing at all, new living quarters to get used to, and having to get used to you! If you've got some complaining to do don't forget to let the conversation go both ways with time, patience and an open mind. Let the people you're caring for vent and get out their complaints as well because it's healthy. The heart-to-heart sessions may also need to be encouraged because it might be difficult for everyone to openly and honestly express their feelings.

There will be a lot that will make you uncomfortable about your caregiving role and there's a lot about your caregiving role that makes the people you care for uncomfortable. For many boomers, after dealing with and reading about all the language from psychologists, therapists, psychiatrists, we know how important it is to express our feelings from our point of concern rather than to place blame. We're all fragile and sensitive and don't appreciate being put down, manipulated, or controlled. Get the conversations started and start them right. Then, get them finished. Use the: I feel..., I'd like to..., I need..., etc., don't place blame by saying: you make me..., you always..., you never.... Ask your loved one to do the same and listen to and respect the responses you get. Make changes so that your environment is more relaxed and happier, one that's more conducive to healing and health and healthy talking and living.

Frustration will indeed rear its head so choose your battles and work to eliminate most of them. If there are discussions that are best had with another person around (a person who is competent and one your loved one likes and trusts) make arrangements to make sure that happens. Be positive during your conversations, talk about a better tomorrow, and make plans.

This is real life until it's over my friends, and there's a fragile, sensitive nature in all of us, whether it's a woman or a man. There's a vanity in us all about who we were, who we are, and what we'll be.

Hint: Good conversations make good vibes and good homes.

Old man hot

He had the swagger of a young man but the face of someone much older who'd seen the sun set on a lot of oceans and had watched it rise again from different doorsteps.

He'd had a lot of drinks and he'd had a lot of laughs and, in the past, had wiped his eyes after saying goodbye to a lot of friends, and to too many lovers. He had children who wouldn't call when he wanted and children who always did whether he wanted them to or not.

Sometimes he wore his clothes a little askew and the older women kissed their teeth and shook their heads from side to side; and sometimes he wore them just right and all the women kissed their teeth and shook their heads — up, and down.

But today, he was just right and winked at me from beneath the wool brim he'd cocked off to the side. He let a smile lift the left side of his lips while "I can still do something for you" eased down the right.

Yeah, like I said, he was an old man.

But he was hot.

And he had a young swagger.

27 Remember To Keep Manners (And Its Cousin, Respect) Close At Hand
Please, never tire of a thank you.

I think the entire world must have sung along when Aretha Franklin first sang out: R-E-S-P-E-C-T. You're both or you're all stressed. You're upset and so are your loved ones. But never get so busy or so stressed that you toss out all manners and forms of respect.

There was a time not long ago when we all used to rely on simple gestures of manners with each other at home, with our friends, and with relatives or total strangers. From 'please pass the pepper' to a simple thank you when the trash is taken out. It seems people now come and go without so much as an 'excuse me' passed between them. It's too easy to allow some of the easiest forms of being mannerly to one another get away from us. People crash into someone in a store or on the street and no one feels the need to say "excuse me". I see men hold doors for women they don't know (and some they do) but I seldom hear the woman acknowledge the gesture with a *thank you*. There are parents who allow their children to run through stores, play and scream in restaurants, and bump into other people without ever reminding or teaching the child to say "excuse me." Manners, from covering your mouth when you cough or sneeze, to chewing with your mouth closed, to, well, you get the point. Keep mannerly behavior in all your relationships. Let others know that you appreciate what they do for you and that manners are important.

Long ago in some far away place and many zip codes before now, I read about the importance of keeping manners in the home between all the people who live in the house, from children to parents and adults to adults. *Mannerly* behavior should be stressed and expected <u>from</u> everybody <u>to</u> everybody, not just outside the home, but inside where it's just as or even more important. I make a point to thank my husband for making the bed and taking out the trash, or when he holds the door open for me. He always thanks me for cooking and says it looks delicious. A little thing, manners, with a positive impact.

I know it seems like childish nonsense, but it isn't. It feels good to be nicer to someone else, so just be mannerly and keep in mind to say "please" and "thank you" to your loved ones, to everyone, and to knock before you enter a room that isn't yours or when the door is closed.

It's time for us to try to soften some of the callousness we've built around ourselves and be more civil to one another. Don't let the caregiving duties and stresses build up so much that respect is lost. Respect privacy. Ask before you lift their clothes or turn them over. Ask to turn off lights, ask if they mind if you stop for visits when you're out together. Ask and be mannerly.

Hint: To borrow from the Big Book: "Do unto others as you would have them do unto you."

Respect your loved ones as the adults and elders they are and demand that everyone in your home do the same. Have conversations regularly with children to ensure that they are being respectful in the words they use and the tone they use when they speak to others. Make certain that visitors are respectful verbally and in their actions.

It's hard giving care either by opening your home to another, moving in to care for someone, or following up with patient care outside your home. Again, it's much harder for those who receive the care. Be mannerly and be respectful in your actions and in your language.

It's just good common sense: Good manners calm trying times.

28 Men and Women Are Different...
...And it has nothing to do with sugar and spice.

Maybe it's because of the 'child birthing' or the natural maternal instincts that some say is innate in most female bodies as the reason more women than men might find themselves in the role of caregiver. I don't know why there are probably more females than males in caregiver roles, but I've heard from some men that they are scared to death and feel all alone when they find themselves in a caregiver role. There is most likely a difference in the feelings men have when they have to give care, but trust me gentlemen, you're not alone. All caregivers feel alone and scared to death.

What I know about this difference comes first hand, as a coach to others in the position of caring, and from male caregivers who have attended my speaking sessions. I don't think a large majority of men are primary caregivers by choice, as is the case with most of the women who take on the role. Women, however, might have other options or other women in the family who may be able to give care. Most women also don't mind crying and getting out their feelings, or asking for help. The men I've talked to aren't able to open up or vent so easily.

Men, I'm telling you now, step up and ask for help. You need the same help, the same tips, the same support as anyone else, and between you and me, I know you might need more because it is different for you — and there's nothing wrong with that.

There are exceptions to everything and I'm not saying that men don't contribute and care for others, or that they don't know how. But just so we can move this along, most women are the nurturers and caregivers for families which includes caring for the men along with the children.

Men and woman move differently through life. Friends are different and defined differently for and by men and men don't want to have the world see them down in any way and sometimes a woman will revel in it. Then there's the protector role that's put on men and when they can't protect they feel they've failed. Caregiving for a loved one must feel like personal failure to you men out there. Well, it does to us 'girls' too.

Men I've known and met seem not to want to be too close to problems and usually, there has been a woman around to get close for them (to make the family phone calls, plan the family get-togethers). When men have to give the care, it's generally to someone who has cared for them.

But it's men taking care of women who must have it pretty strange and can make a man feel unsettled. I see women taking care of men with colds, women who bandage men's cuts and get aspirin for their headaches. I hear about women who make the meals and manage the home and then get to the office. These women are taking care of men, women, and sometimes children. Some men might find themselves at a disadvantage when, or if, they have to do the full time cooking, house management, be the chauffeur and cargiver for a loved one who was very good at taking care of them.

You may also find that it isn't easy for you to care for your female mate because we aren't easy people. Maybe the females have been the ones to tell you how much medicine to take, put the food on your plate, got dressed up for you, looked good for you. Now its different. You find they've hidden secrets from you with the unending uplifts, hair coloring, manicures, hip and stomach control from spandex, and plucking and tweezing and your shocked. Women will undress in front of sisters, mothers, and girlfriends to compare notes and ask questions, so a lot of us girls have seen it before, but their husbands and boyfriends probably have to fight to get their women to disrobe in front of them and don't know the secrets. This is a whole new way of looking at love for both of you, but love it still is.

I stick with my observations: men and women are different but both can give good care. In a world where a man is usually expected to be in control or able to take charge, here comes caregiving and it all changes. Men, reach out and ask questions. Reach out to a good friend and have a serious conversation if you can, or contact your pastor or call an 800 phone line for advice or someone to talk to about the position you're in, the new situation for you. Find better (healthier) take out spots to augment the cooking so you don't have to do so much of that "kitchen stuff" and keep friends at the ready for you and your loved one, especially for your loved one for the personal upkeep she may well be concerned about. Keep water, beverages, hot tea, fruit, wheat bread, hard candies, and large soap available for your loved one. And men, get yourselves to as many caregiver support sessions as you can. When you get there, talk it up!

It's as tough for the female caregivers as it is for you men, and every caregiver doubts themselves every day. Maybe we women just make it look too simple.

Chapter VII

SHALL WE DANCE?

29 Remember the Importance of Music In Your Life and the Life of Your Loved One
Let music be part of your therapy.
Turn it up and move something!

A couple of years ago when I spoke to a caregivers' group, I talked about the importance of putting music back in the lives of caregivers and in the lives of the loved ones they care for. What I knew and believed then about the benefits of music hasn't changed. What has changed is that finally, music has been highly recognized to be the therapeutic benefit most of us boomers have relied on through the years.

Researchers at hospitals say long-term pain suffers have significant pain relief and less depression after listening to music of their own choice for one hour. At Harvard's Institute for Music and Brain Science, Dr. Tramo explains music can cause changes in the specific parts of the brain that are related to the body's feel good systems. And at Berklee School of Music in Boston, Dr. Suzanne Hanser heads a program that will introduce music therapy to reduce anxiety, depression and the negative effects of other illnesses as part of long-term care for patients.

Across the country, hospitals and day care centers for adults and children, are incorporating music into their programs to encourage healing, stimulate coma patients or to soothe patients and visitors.

And it isn't just music that's been found to be beneficial, it's the sound of a melodic voice that's speaking and voices singing together with or without music, or participating in the arts in general: like visiting museums, attending plays, and spending time for creative efforts. It all aids in a better life and has been shown to directly improve the quality of life for patients.

My tip to you is to remember the importance of keeping music in your life and in the life of your loved one.

I can appreciate the newspaper and magazine articles I read that announce these findings about music as though they're new. But the fact is, and any boomer worth their weight will tell you, music has played a healing part in their lives and their parents' lives for years and years. Have you ever lost a love? Maybe you've put on Smokey Robinson singing, "OOO Baby Baby." If there's a new love for you, Luther Vandross could be what you pop on. Want to feel totally empowered? Play and sing out loudly the words to any song by Luciano Pavaratti. If you need to relax and calm down, try the smooth saxophone of Kenny G.

From years past and into the present, there has been a host of super musicians and vocalists who have helped us make it through the night. Jerry Butler, The Four Tops, The Righteous

Brothers, The Manhattans, Bread, Creedence Clearwater Revival, Frank Sinatra, Jimmy Hendrix, Sly and the Family Stone, The Temptations, Blood, Sweat, and Tears, Phoebe Snow, Rare Earth, Santana, The O'Jays, The Beetles, The Jackson Five, and on and on and on it goes. There are so many great groups, singers and sounds that helped the generation of boomers through, that's it's too long a list to go into right now.

While growing up in my parents' house there was music from Broadway tunes, to jazz, to country, to blues and R&B. My parents had music they used specifically for getting dressed for parties, music for the parties, and even close the party down music. Music has been there since the beginning of our growing up and has been the background of our busy, lively, dedicated, and tumultuous lives.

Music has been the soother, settler, and the entertainer of our in- and out-of-love times, the fights and battles in our lives, and our beat for simply cleaning up our rooms and doing our chores. We've cried to it, danced to it, and let our moods go high and low with it. There is no way you can, and no reason you should, eliminate it now. As a matter of fact, now more than ever you need music and your loved ones need it, too.

The positive impact has been made clear on this through the years and there's no question about it: Good music is like good food — it just makes a body and a home feel better. The trick is to make sure it's music your loved one likes when you're playing it for them and music you like when you're playing it for yourself, because for any individual, I believe bad music has the reverse effect of good music.

When you know what you want, then dig the tapes or albums out of storage, go out and buy it, or order the music you want online. It's never been easier to get what you want. You can go on-line to iTunes and Amazon.com or take a trip to Circuit City or Best Buy. AARP also has a new site at www.aarp.org/music, an online streaming music service. If you aren't computer savvy, find someone who is (another chance to let people do what they do and help you out) who can download the songs you want. I'm not getting paid by any of these places, I just know them to be useful. One store I'll gladly support is George's Music Room in Chicago, Illinois. They have nearly anything you can think of and will order what they don't have. George (who has made a name for himself through his profound quote: "Music is memories and emotions" and his video appearances) also knows about music. I've called his store with only a melody on my mind to find out the name of the artist attached to it. Off the tip of his tongue, or one of the music mavens working with him, the artist's name rolls.

The music you want is out there. Get it and play it, heal to it, dance to it, and relax to it.

30 Play the Music Then Watch and Listen
Stories really know how to dance to the tunes.

Some of my fathers' favorite performers past and present are Tommy Edwards, Julie London, Gladys Knight, the Stylistics, and Nat King Cole. Actually, the Stylistics should be first. I know what music both my parents like, what my sister likes, and what my husband likes, with or without them needing care. But if you don't know what music the people you're caring for like, ask them.

I've heard and read that people with dementia might not re-member what happened to them five minutes ago but will re-member verbatim the words of songs and the melody of music they loved from 50 years ago. Because of this revelation, assisted living homes and senior centers in many cities are incorporating music in everyday situations and in their entertainment sched-ules for the residents. Music is background for dinner, foreground for dances where the residents are the act, and even audible while the Wii for exercise creeps into senior centers.

Around the country, music is being introduced for relaxation, entertainment, and to get patients and residents active and in-volved. In Avarda, Colorado near Denver, there's a group called Swinging Seniors who meet for music and dancing. An 87-year old man plays the accordion, an 84-year old man is on keyboards and along with violinists Mary Lou, 86, and Ed, 81, they 'kick it'. They play the music, the crowd dances, everyone shares stories about their pasts, and someone will sing along.

Musically inclined residents and participants with numerous ailments and from diverse backgrounds are participating in mu-sic night and rocking the house in day centers and living facili-ties. From singing to playing the instruments to simply dancing and enjoying the music, the sick and the young and old are ben-efiting from the power of music and stories about lives lived are being told to the beats. Music is bringing good feelings, good moods, good memories, and a sense of purpose back to the young and old, sick and well.

I can tell you first hand that music and dementia are not friends! My mother-in-law had Alzheimers, and like many pa-tients with that disease she kept up the battle of pretense, pretending to know everyone and everything around her. When music was played she didn't have to pretend any more. During one of the evening events at my husband's family reunion years ago, I danced with my mother-in-law for hours. Not only could she and did she dance, but she knew the words to most of the songs—which were, I have to say, a good mix of current and old tunes that I'd put together for the event. We literally closed the place down!

For all the bad it does, dementia had no idea that music would stay in the mind and provide so much enjoyment. In an article edited by Drs. Ladislav Volicer and Lisa Bloom-charette, we're told that many with dementia are able to maintain rhythmic abilities and that meaningful music triggers functional activity and emotions. They also point out that individual preference (again, I say, play what you like and what your loved one likes) is important for the music to have a positive effect.

At 85 years old, Mr. Tell can't remember yesterday but he still plays the piano and has 3,000 songs in his mind. He plays at the Memory Café, a floating club in Colorado underwritten by HealthONE Alliance and the Alzheimer's Association of Colorado for people suffering memory loss, their families, and their caregivers. After listening to Al Tell play Chattenooga Choo-Choo, one resident said, "I've danced thousands of miles to that song."

One of the most memorable times I spent with my grandmother was during an afternoon of music and talking. I'd decided it was time to get some stories from her and have her fill in some blanks about our family history as best she could. My grandmother was a consummate storyteller and could weave a tale as well as she was able to (at one time) weave a stitch. It was during an afternoon when she was feeling pretty good and had no leg cramps and no headache, and was ready for some of her favorite foods that had been cooked for dinner that I felt it was a good time. I sat down next to her and put on the stereo, took out my tape recorder and asked her about the first man she ever loved. With the sound of the music in the background, Gram moved her feet to the beat and rattled off stories about people and places she'd known and started the story about the first time she'd seen my grandfather. I enjoyed every expression that came across her face and I could see that the music really relaxed and entertained her. She moved, which she should have done more of, and she smiled, which I'm sorry she couldn't do more of, and she looked like, in spite of it all, she was having a good time. Yes, good music.

Don't wait any longer. Make music, the music your loved one is partial to, a part of their day or at least a part of the week. Let the music play while you're cooking or cleaning, while finishing up those hobbies, while you and your loved one are relaxing. Play the music to take the mind off the illness and see if the therapy really works to lessen the pain. Let it enliven the walls of your house and give people a reason to tap their feet, tell some stories about their lives, and hum a tune. Take your pick and offer the choice: R&B, classical, rock, country, rap, easy listening. It all works if it's what makes you both (all) feel good. I have to remind you, if music is bad for you it's bad for your body and mind, not just your ears. Play what feels good to everyone or make music available on a room-by-room basis or use your earphones when you've got to hear what you've got to hear. While the music is playing, get the video, get a recorder and get down those stories.

I have good memories of my Gram, telling the stories and enjoying the music. Me, dancing the night away with my mother-in-law. I'm thrilled with the stories I read about people across the country feeling better and feeding their spirit with music. I'm telling you, don't let these times pass you by. Play the music then watch and listen!

#31 Aaah, Love
Remember the significance of at least four kinds of love.

Aaah, love: Love for yourself, love for the one you love, love for the one you're caring for, and their love for someone else. There are so many different kinds of love that there's no time to list them all here. For now, I want to remind you about the importance of remembering the four kinds of love that should be in our lives and the significance of giving each one of them the time and space they deserve.

Caregivers: don't forget to love yourself. We all know it and we all forget it but now more than ever when you're giving so much time and energy to others, you've got to stop and love you. You can talk about taking giant steps that you might not be able to afford or find the time for, or you can think about and take some simple steps, like giving yourself a pat on the back and taking *you* shopping. Love yourself and walk off the stress or love you and join a dance class. Be easy enough on yourself and kind enough to yourself to do what you can to rebuild yourself. Love yourself, be gentle on yourself and on your mistakes.

One thing that's always good is to try to relax your entire body at some point during the day. I once read that only cats and infants are capable of totally relaxing their bodies and since you don't fall into that category, it will take more than just the act of sitting down in order to totally relax.

For full body relaxation, I've read that you should lie down (back or stomach doesn't matter, on my back is my preference) and then concentrate on every part of your body. Start with your head or face, and relax it. Clear your thoughts, stop frowning, stop clenching your jaws and just relax. Move on to your shoulders, arms, hands, hips, thighs, legs, and feet and let each body part relax and ease down on the bed or the floor. One body part at a time should hold your attention until you have released the tension from each of the muscles along the way, each part of your body that deserves to relax. You know me, so you know that I want you to add some soothing background music but I also understand and can appreciate the gift of silence, so if you prefer to let the silence take over, do, if it works better for you. However you choose to relax, in the tub, on the floor, or on a break at your desk, try to totally relax your body—and hopefully, your mind will follow.

Make sure you make time for romance and love with your mate. Love didn't move out of the heart just because a situation changed in the house. You still need the hugs and the kisses and the sweet talk about love that has nothing to do with caregiving. Don't let your caregiving duties make you fall out of love. If you weren't in love, maybe you can think about getting into it. Now more than ever, you need the touch, tenderness, and warmth of love. Make time for it so you don't get bitter or full with the feeling that you've given all of yourself away to caring for someone else. Those feelings will only cause resentment and hatred, and quite honestly, who needs those feelings? Wrap yourself in the love of your mate or a fine friend. Give a hug and a kiss just because it's three o'clock in the afternoon, make those middle-of-the-day calls that have nothing to do with work, celebrate something with and for the mate you love, and when you're close to each other, put your heads on each others' shoulders. You'll feel better mentally and physically when you reach out and let love reach back. Take it it's yours.

If you're caring for your mate, your needs and sentiments are vast and there may be difficulty in finding love with them. You'll have to remember the love and if there's the chance, look forward to it coming back to you like it once was. You'll have to use other arms of family and friends to hold you, but make sure you find time to give hugs and kisses to your mate to help calm you and them down. Touch is important to all humans.

> Hint: Loving you is about keeping your love spirit alive.

Another kind of love is one that has got to be shown to the people you care for. Since the love for them is one that's filled with so many other emotions and responsibilities that have been added, it gets easy to simply go through the motions and think the people you're giving care to know you love them just because you're there. But just as it's possible that you don't feel loved or appreciated after all your caregiving responsibilities, the people you're caring for might not feel the love from you, either. You and the person you're caring for still have to show your love for one another. Make some changes to lighten things up and bring easy, casual, delightful, heartfelt love back in the picture.

How about this for easy? You should, and can, laugh more together. No matter the situation, find something to laugh about. Do it because it's good for you and do it because it will ease tension and add a bond that makes you both feel more loved. There's more about laughter in tip #34.

Every month there's some "Hallmark" holiday that's been created in order for them to sell more cards. Buy some of them if you want or just do something special to celebrate the times that mean something to you and yours. Find some obscure dates and history events and use them to make some special moments or make up your own special dates: second Saturday for hobby time, around-the-world dinner-night on the second Thursday every other month, new-movie night one Sunday a month with no interruptions. Get creative and celebrate the time. Show your love in easy ways.

You can show your love by exercising together, cooking together ("Nothin' says loving like something from the oven..."), relaxing together, or keeping busy together.

Talk about keeping busy! People are getting out and transporting what they need on the road with them. And the stigmas that were once attached to all the accoutrements are now obsolete. I've seen people in clubs and theatres with oxygen tanks, in wheel chairs, on canes, and in casts, all out and about. Take a trip to a casino and you'll see what I mean. My point and the importance of it is that you find something to do together like you used to do or that you've wanted to do together, and you'll show your love. Maybe you can play board games. They're still great mind extenders, inexpensive, good for group activity and great for the sick, shut-in, or for starting a new weekly tradition.

Make time to relax a little together. Go to the beach during the day or at night and watch and listen to the ocean. Enjoy the sun at the beach or enjoy the moonlight and the people traffic. Head to the mountains or a national park. Beaches and parks are plentiful and most are free to enjoy and are underused. Use them as often as you can. Relax in the park with some of the papers or some of the magazine articles you haven't had a chance to read. No beaches or parks for you to take advantage of with your loved ones? Then make a few (or pick up some) sandwiches from the supermarket and just sit outside on your deck, on your patio or on your stoop, laugh a lot and welcome neighbors or friends who might pass by and see you out. Loosen up a bit in your home and talk about good things, fun things, light hearted things. Cooking is another great activity to get involved in so you're together in a more relaxed and caring way. Bake cookies and give them away. Well, don't give them all away.

Showing your love for each other in ways that are filled with activity or by being more relaxed will go a long way in easing your stresses and the stresses of your loved ones.

Another kind of love is the love your loved one has for their other children and relatives. This is where I get to tell everyone that sibling rivalry and trying to make decisions on what you think another heart should hold has no place in caregiving and should be put in a box, a burden basket, or just tossed out of your mind.

It's no surprise to anyone that those who do the cargiving might feel they should get all or most of the love of their loved one. But it, love and how it's dispensed, just doesn't work that way. None of us has any way of knowing what kind of love other people share with each other or the depth of it. It isn't ours to know. Your job as the caregiver should be to do the best you can to make every effort to include, in some way, as many of the people your loved one loves.

If you're caring for a parent or parents and have siblings who are at a distance, those siblings will probably feel like long-distance caregivers whether they're giving physical care or not. Find ways to include the other children by giving them chores and responsibilities they can manage from a distance and encourage them to show their love in whatever way they can and at every opportunity they get. Visits, or simply cards and letters (yes, the real things that need postage stamps) feel good in the hands of your loved ones and are great for them to put on their nightstands. E-mails and telephone calls work wonders, too. Parents have a great capacity for love to and for each of their children, so don't let jealousy, old arguments, old rivalries, or stubbornness and control make you shut out the other children or other relatives your loved ones love.

You, dear caregiver, are not the appointed host of the heart because you decided to give care or the responsibility of giving the care is with you. It's tough and maybe you think it isn't fair, but your loved one holds love for other family members even though you're the one giving the care. Open up and let in the love and you and your loved one will feel better.

Lastly, there's the love your loved one has for their lovers past or present. For some caregivers it might be hard to address or to be honest about the past or current physical love of your loved one if you're caring for parents, other older relatives or friends, or older children. But I really want you to understand that your loved one is, or probably has been, in love. Somewhere way down deep, love sits or stands up and jogs the memory about how it used to be. There is also, most likely, some unfulfilled, unrequited, and unfinished love hanging around in their heart. Their present or current situation will only magnify the idea of loves loved or lost because they have more time to think back and about it. If you're lucky in your caregiver case, mates are still together. If they aren't, maybe you've been privy to some of the stories about loved ones who are no longer together. Either way, there will always be details you will know nothing about. You have got to remember that physical and emotional love is or has existed for the person you're caring for and that it just enriches the tapestry of their life making it more dramatic and complex. Depending on the situation, allow privacy for love and loving moments, encourage new love relationships, and help ease the emotional turmoil of losing love.

When I coach caregivers or those being cared for, one or both miss love in some way. Because of that, I always include a poem about love when I speak to groups of caregivers, both to get my point across and to best illustrate the depth love can take. These pieces were inspired by my grandparents and the aunt and uncle of a dear friend.

Burt...

In his dreams
He would walk up to the woman he hadn't seen in too many years
and gaze down at the cinnamon colored silk stockings that lived like sunset along
the calves of her fine, fine legs.
He'd get close enough to smell the cologne on the pulse of her neck
if the wind was kind and lifted the fragrance to him.
It was in those dream moments that he'd wrap his heavy heart around the hope
that,
maybe,
she still loved him.

...and Anna

She could always hear him - from somewhere in the night -
after the neighborhood had settled to sleep
and the house had quieted from its wood and stone noises.
The essence of him would lean down and whisper a soft hello into the ear
that had longed,
for so long,
to hear the touch of his voice.

Mae and Ira

He woke for no particular reason in that middle of the night,
sat up and took hold of Mae's slender ninety-five year old shoulders.
He held her tight and kissed her between her lips with all the passion and
strength of his
ninety-seven years.
He told her quite simply, he'd always loved her and he always would.

Then, Ira lay back down in their bed beside his wife,
with no more to say
and no breath left in his body
and went to sleep for the rest of Mae's life.

He took with him two hearts that had lived and loved together for seventy-nine
years
and she
shook her head and marveled at how time flies.

32 Don't Forget to Include the Friends — (Yours and Theirs)
They're called friends for a reason.

Remember earlier when I espoused all the stuff about facing the facts, being honest, and creating peaceful arrangements while incorporating these tips? Well, here's another chance for you to take the time to put honesty and facing facts into action. This is about the dynamics that go beyond the relationship of you and your loved one. This is about not forgetting your friends or theirs and in the case of your loved ones, being honest about who their friends really are.

We all pretty much know who we like, which personalities we're attracted to, which people comfort us, challenge us, make us laugh and make us happy when we see them come into a room and which ones have us searching for the highest wall to climb and make us feel better when they leave. This isn't about giving the benefit of the doubt to all the people who have caused problems with our loved ones or with us (which, we know, ultimately means, with our loved ones) so it doesn't have a place here. This is about the people who are honest-to-goodness make-you-feel-good friends. You need them and you have got to make sure you find a way to keep them in your and your loved ones' life.

Don't forget your friends. Friends feed our spirits with their unique personalities and clever ways of making light of our troubles and the way they reach out and "wrap us in spontaneous hugs." Having real friends around is very important to our health, our quality of life and our wellbeing. You probably have one friend to cook with, one to head to a football game with, one you can count on for keeping your secrets, and one who knows your past and all your truths. Whatever your list of friends is like, keep in touch with as many of them as you can. Get dressed up and visit your friends, give a get-together and have them over, meet for drinks and laugh off some calories, give an old-fashioned card party and give it in the afternoon — you've got to take off some time from work, anyway.

With all the friends you have or out of the few you have, there might be one particular friend who is difficult for others to understand, appreciate or bear. The 'others' happen to be your loved one who lives with you. Try to schedule time with these friends when you can appreciate their uniqueness by yourself. In short, schedule time with your unique friends so that others don't have to be bothered by them. Keep it real and keep it honest. All people don't like the same people.

Don't forget to include the friends of your loved ones. I think it's of utmost importantance for you to do what you can to get your loved ones or the people you're caring for together with their friends and arrange for them to get together as often as possible. For the positive impact your friends have for you in good or bad times, remember the impact the friends of your loved one must have on them. Keep in mind that contact with old friends, true friends, will lift them up and satisfy them on different levels.

My grandmother was a gregarious person and had friends she'd known and socialized with for nearly seventy years before illness forced her to have to leave her home. In her neighborhood she knew everyone from one end of her street (a long street) to the other. When she was able, she'd walk her neighborhood and visit friends to drop off a little something for them, make social calls to newer friends, and special visits to those who were sick and shut in. One of the things she missed most about having to leave her old neighborhood were the friends she'd had. One of them, Mrs. Allen, who had lived across the hall from Gram, had been out of town when my grandmother was moved out of her house and to Queens. Gram often asked me to get in touch with Mrs. Allen so she'd know where Gram was. I couldn't reach Mrs. Allen and it always troubled me to know that the two of them, who had been friends for so many years, were separated with neither knowing where the other was.

The history your loved one has with their friends is one that should be valued. Do whatever you can to either find the friends of your loved ones, or the family members of the friends and exchange information. Insist that your loved one contact their friends so that the relationship can continue.

If you find that your loved ones' calls to friends aren't returned, investigate because it's possible that good care or conditions aren't prevalent on the other side. Contact a decent friend or family member of that person or elder law or social services. With all the change you and your loved ones have encountered, some things don't need to and shouldn't change. Be instrumental in keeping the friendships alive.

Since there are opposites for everything, there are friends and there are enemies, both of whom might also be relatives. Guidelines are usually clear for what constitutes a friend but what constitutes an enemy and who they are may be cloaked by the family crest and denial. For some reason, a few people will turn a blind eye to blatant lies or misdeeds.

If for example, your cousin or your uncle have never liked being around Aunt Mary, or the seemingly pleasant friends or children of an ex-mate, there's probably a darn good reason for it whether you're aware of it or not. And if your Mom and Dad have always enjoyed the company of their neighbors from around the block or friends from their church but not the visits from your nephew, now might not be the time to force a change. For the person you're caring for and for your well being, try — as hard as it is — to bear in mind who are the friends and who are the enemies and to keep the friends close and the enemies, in this instance, further away.

Face the fact that every single family in the world comes from a foundation that includes some kind of disagreement, unpleasantness, and drama, and that what has to be done now is to keep the drama at bay. Don't bring it around your loved ones purposely or deliberately. Remember the friends, yours and theirs, and the enemies, yours and theirs.

If reaching old friends isn't an option or if many good friends of your loved one have passed away, it's never too late to find new friends for yourself or your loved one. It might be less difficult for you to meet new people than it is for your loved one if they've been uprooted and are in a new location, are much older, shut-in, or depressed. The difficulty will be compounded if they are really introverts at heart. Find ways for the people you care for to meet people and make new friends. It might be as simple as taking a trip to the mall.

During the question and talk-it-out sessions at the end of one of my lectures to caregivers, a woman asked what she could do to stimulate and engage her 92-year old mother. She mentioned that her mother, who lived with her, was a little frail but primarily a healthy person, used to be extremely active and had always enjoyed playing the piano and socializing in diverse settings. She also told the audience that she'd given her mother paper dolls so that she could entertain herself and keep busy.

I told her to give the paper dolls to one of the children in the neighborhood and get her mother dressed in a good outfit and out and around people her age who had parallel interests, were sophisticated, and continued to be active. I told her to take her mother to the mall.

Ironically, the day before my talk I'd read a story in the daily paper about a 90-year-old man who frequented the local mall. During his interview with the writer he said he enjoyed regular trips to the mall where he was able to exercise freely by taking walks around the inside without having to worry about the weather. After his indoor walk, he would stop and to socialize and was encouraged to play the piano that was in the mall for use by all serious pianists. He said it was a great way to spend his time and that he'd derived a great deal of joy from meeting new people who would come up to him and just strike up conversations. He was shocked he said, at how easy it had been for him to make new friends. I believe he went on to say that a lot of people his age didn't want to get out but they didn't know what they were missing.

They're called friends for a reason and they are spirit feeders one and all. One to cook with, one to laugh with, one for sharing secrets, one who knows the past, one who knows your truth and true self, some to share your thoughts of the day and some to share thoughts about tomorrow. Friends are people providing purpose. I either read it or heard it said recently that "friends are as good as Prozac" and it's so true. They seem to lift our burdens right off our shoulders.

Find like-spirits for your loved one and encourage a social life for them independent of you.

Chapter **VIII**

A WORD TO THE WISE

#33 Don't Fertilize the Small Stuff and It Probably Won't Grow
Choose your battles.

This is simple: manage your emotions, keep anger under control and keep the worry at bay. Don't take setbacks personally and learn to practice self-discipline for your tongue. As caregivers you will have to make a conscious effort to choose how you'll respond to different situations and to different people that you will come in contact with on a regular basis, many more than those who aren't involved in caregiving. You'll have to be diplomatic and aggressive to get answers and information from hospital workers, doctors, health organizations, landlords other than your own, mortgage companies and lawyers other than your own, community organizations, ambulance drivers, and maybe some relatives you've never seen. Because your network has broadened and widened since you started giving care, the potential for your battlefields to have also grown is undeniable. This new, broader network may make you short on patience and could make it easy for you to dwell on the small stuff that has nothing to do with the big picture.

Choose your battles carefully in and out of your home and whatever you do, don't push buttons that aggravate, anger, and annoy. Don't argue about nonsense from months ago or spilled milk from days ago. Pick your battles carefully because your energy has to travel in a number of directions and you don't want to have your loved one feel disrespected, unloved, or that they're a burden to you because of a bad day you're having. And since this is always a two-way street of people pushing buttons, don't allow anyone to push yours.

Stop fertilizing worries. Let go of worries over which you have no control because for one, most of our worries are fabricated. They are pretty much ones we create. We worry about what might happen in the future or what could have happened in the past. There is also the worry we commit ourselves to that involves the past and what can't be changed. I've heard that only 15% of what we worry about is worthy of our attention and of that, maybe only 5% is within our control to fix. But real or imagined, worries cause anxiety and stress that triggers a reaction to situations, and usually the reaction is not as positive as it should be. It isn't easy, and even as I'm writing this for each of you, I'm trying to put some excessive worry out my mind as well. It's always a struggle to practice what we preach!

Friends, we can't be everywhere and do everything. Having healthy routines, talking to good friends, getting a lot of love, being dedicated to honesty, playing good music, being kind to the sensitive natures of others and getting help from people will help you stay unflappable and productive through high-pressure periods. It will help you to choose your battles and toss out the bad stuff fertilizer.

34 Laughter Really Is Good Medicine!
Laugh like you know nothing lasts forever
(cry for the very same reason).

On a recent segment of Good Morning America, a doctor shared findings that laughter lowers blood pressure, increases circulation, soothes tension, wakes up the feel good hormones (endorphins) and is good for heart health. He said that the studies suggest the body doesn't know the difference between real aerobic activity and laughter, and that one minute of laughter is the equivalent of six minutes of exercise (ha, ha, ha, ha, ha, ad infinitum!). Laughter engages all systems in the mind and body.

Laugh like you know nothing lasts forever. When did we stop laughing so hard and so often at each other, at bad jokes, and at ourselves? Now more than ever with world news the way it is and these new changes and challenges set before caregivers in particular—laugh. Laugh at a movie, laugh about a recipe gone wrong, laugh at yourself, laugh at a mistake, but laugh. It's good medicine. Burn those calories, lower your pressure and change your mood!

If you find it too hard to get the laughter rolling and you're in a pinch, try smiling. It's good for you and yours and works from the outside in. It will make you feel better because you're putting forth the effort and anyone who looks your way will feel better, too.

These days, you probably wear worry, fatigue, and sadness on your face more often than you realize. Now, take that look (the sad one you've earned because of all you're going through, violins here, please) to the mirror and pay attention: 'smile and the world smiles with you.' Lift up the ends of those lips and help the person staring back at you to feel better. Wear the smile to make a phone call and let another person hear the smile in your voice. It's contagious and they'll smile, too. Then, take that same smile and copy it so you have another one handy because I know how hard it may have been to get one in the first place. Now go in to see your loved one, plan to visit with the smile on, or get in touch with a smile in your voice. Leave the extra smile with them to help make their day better and brighter. They may not want it immediately, but put it on their forehead wrapped in a kiss, or on their cheek, or on the dresser or just leave it at the foot of their bed. At some point during their day, they'll pick it up and possibly put it on and pass it along. It may even come back to you later in the day. But most definitely, they'll be glad it's there.

#35 Give Your Best Self Whenever and Wherever You Give Care
It will shine through forever.

Everybody, every caregiver out there, I'm talking to you. You've got a job to do. Wherever and whenever you give care, give your best, whether it's in your home, in the home or residence of your loved one, or while they're in the hospital. The age of the person you're caring for doesn't matter, your age doesn't matter, and it doesn't matter if they're related to you or not. They need for you to be responsible. You are needed to bolster the confidence of your loved one. You are required to make certain they are getting the best medical care. It is imperative that you encourage their independence. You have to add bright spots to their days and nights and plan for better tomorrows. You are needed (as a sibling not a dictator) to coordinate time spent and keep everyone involved. You are needed to be honest, to take care of yourself, to be respectful of their situation, to feed their spirit, and to keep your prayers strong and add music to their life.

When all else fails, and sometimes it will, your responsibility will be to sit down and have a tall glass of ice water, a short mohito, a dry white wine, or get up and do the Electric Slide.

> Hint: Feed and nurture the human spirit because
> In the end, it's all we've got.

Chapter IX

To the Caregiver
Give back to you because it's your life, too.

You might have moments when you feel there's no end in sight and you're right-- there isn't. Whatever your duties might be, you sandwiched between your children and your parents or elders, you caring for a loved one who lives far away, you adjusting to the demands of a loved one who needs care in your home, or you being the only one to take dinner to your neighbor — you are in demand.

You are so much in demand and involved in the lives of others that you may have forgotten that more than one life is at stake: yours and theirs. Maybe it has slipped your mind that it's your life, too.

With that in mind, let me just close my tips to you by streaming some final thoughts your way. They're just a few hints peppered with common sense.

Give back to you because it's your life, too.

Dear Caregiver,

You do great things for those you love, but you're human. There are no saints working around here. Take some time out for you.

You've still got to live your life — no one wants you to give up everything for them (and you're no fun when you do!).

You've lifted, pushed, pulled, measured, cried, walked up, walked down, walked away and answered the call and that's just in one day. You've got to be tired. When fatigue comes — and it will — rest.

Some hamburger-serving goliath said it long ago and it stuck: "You deserve a break today..." To that I have to add: When you take a break you give everybody else a break, and they need one from you!

If you don't get away and give everyone some private space, the entire house will go crazy. For the peace of mind of all concerned you've got to put a little distance between you and caregiving. Take a walk, take a ride, take a weekend, but take a break.

Do something different or do something old a different way. Take a new way to work, walk a new walk or walk that old walk like you used to; tell a new joke or an old story with a different voice, and sing along loud and strong with the music you love. Do it just for you.

Get dressed up again and add your good jewelry. Find your enjoyment.

Remember that the person you're caring for feels worse than you.

Get up earlier than the household to find some time for yourself. And it will have to be very early because you know that sick people and old people get up very early.

Keep asking for your loved ones to do what they need to do to better their situations, but stop begging. I've said it before and here it is again: people don't change, situations do.

Remember the blessings you have and remember those blessings to brighten your way.

We try to (more tossing good grammar aside) do good, be good, and act good but we're all just human.

Love your strongest and give your the best from your heart wanting nothing in return.

Pray. Pray for yourself and for those you love. Pray for us all.

There's a lot within our control, but ultimately, the control is not ours.

REFERENCES

1. Woodstock: A rock music festival held in 1969 near Woodstock, New York

2. Change Gone Come, written by Sam Cooke, produced by Hugo Peretti and Luigi Creatore, RCA Victor Records, 1965.

5. For various reasons, numbers cannot be calculated accurately. They appear in broad ranges in various articles and broadcasts and range in the millions up to 44 million.

6. MSNBC, 24-hour cable news channel in the United States and Canada; msnbc.com

6. USA Today, a division of Gannett Co., Inc.

9. Stylistics, The Stylistics, Stop, Look, Listen to Your Heart Hear What it's Saying, 1987

11. Willard Scott's segment on ABC Good Morning America, presented by Smucker's, The J.M. Smucker Company

13. New nursing homes geared to ethnicity, 'A Better Life' USA Today, October 13, 2004.

17. High cost of caregiving, equivalent of $350 billion in 2006; Source: AARP

18. EEOC.gov; worklifelaw.org; nationalpartnership.org; Balancing Act by Maggie Jackson, Boston Sunday Globe, July 15, 2007

Note: Also visit: www.eldercare.gov, Rocky Mountain News, November 1, 2004; www.aarp.org/families, USA Today, June 25, 2007

33. 'Lively Up Yourself' written by Bob Marley and Peter Tosh; produced by Chris Blackwell and The Wailers, 1973.

34. Diana Ross, 'It's My House' written by Nicholas Ashford and Valerie Simpson, 1979

36. Shoji screens: Three-panel screens used as a room divider.

39. 'Harvard doc's study says flowers brighten moods, as well as rooms, Nancy L. Etcoff by Marie Szaniszlo, Saugus Advertiser, 2006 Nancy Etcoff w/flowers

40. Feng shui: a Chinese system that studies people's relationships to their environments.

40. 'Frasier', Television program with Kelsey Grammer. Aired September 1993-May 2004; Grub Street Productions, originally NBC

41. 'The Good, the Bad, and the Ugly' starring Clint Eastwood, released 1997, United Artists

41. Temptations, R&B singing group, originally with Motown Records, 'For Lovers Only' by the Temptations, UMG Recordings, Inc., a division of Motown, 2002.

41,42. USA Today, March 2000, Dr. Carter w/ et. al, discusses usefulness of light for elders Lighting designs for aging eyes: Dr. Alan Lewis, president of the New England College of Optometry; Peter Boyce, professor, Rensselaer Polytechnic

Institute; www.asaging.org; www.lrc.rpi.edu/ Projects/ elderly.html.

46. Best Foods Mayonnaise, sold as Hellman's east of the
Mississippi; a Unilever product

46. Jif Peanut Butter, made by The J.M. Smucker co.

50. "...forget your sickness and dance..." from 'Them Belly Full
(But We Hungry),' written by Bob Marley, credited to Vincent
Ford; produced by Chris Blackwell and The Wailers, 1974.

52. House & Garden Television, High Noon Productions, Inc.;
HGTV If Walls Could Talk

52. Oprah, The Oprah Winfry Show, Harpo Productions, Inc.

61. Billy Ocean, 'Caribbean Queen', written by Billy Ocean and
Robert John "Mutt" Lange; co-produced by Robert John
"Mutt" Lange; Jive Records 1984

69. Native American Smudge bundles/ sticks, white sage, cedar,
sweet grass, used, for example, to cleanse space.

71. 'Sit and be Fit' with Mary Ann Wilson, a senior exercise and
senior fitness television series; PBS broadcast

Note: Also see, 'Rise and Shine' with Ann Smith, Scott Craig
Productions, Inc., 2001

76. Chris Rock, comedian, HBO special 'Never Scared', 2004,
Home Box Office Cablevision Network

77. 'The Pharmacist Who Says No to Drugs' by Armon Neel,
AARP Bulletin, September 2004

79. Marion Meadows Dressed to Chill, written by Michael
Broening, produced by Michael Broening, 2006, Heads

Up International.

89. 'Old Man Hot', Excerpt from More for the Heart of Your Soul, Sweet Tea and hot Coffee, Sandra Jackson, PJ's Publishing, 2008

90. Aretha Franklin 'R-e-s-p-e-c-t', written by Otis Redding, produced by Jerry Wexler; Atlantic Records, 1967

91. The Big Book, 'Do Unto Others...' also referred to as the Golden Rule, from The Book of Matthew, 7:12, Sermon on the Mount, The Bible

98. Harvard's Institute for Music and Brain Science, Mark Jude Tramo, M.D., Ph.D., HealthyUpdates.com

98. 'OOO Baby Baby' written by William 'Smokey' Robinson and Warren Pete Moore, produced by William 'Smokey' Robinson, Tamla Records, 1965

100. George's Music Room in Chicago, Illinois

101. Seniors in Arvada; 'Seniors savor music, kind words, hugs', by Gary Massaro, The Rocky Mountain News, November 22, 2005

102. Mr. Tell from 'Music and dementia; Man's life in the 'music he remembered', by Gary Massaro, The Rocky Mountain News, 2005

106. Hallmark Cards, the largest maker of greeting cards.

107. "Nothin' says lovin' like something from the over and Pillsbury says it best..."; Vintage jingle from the Pillsbury Company

111. 'Bert', Excerpt from For the Heart of Your Soul, Sandra

Jackson, PJ's Publishing, 2000

111. 'Anna', Excerpt from For the Heart of Your Soul, Sandra Jackson, PJ's Publishing, 2000

112. 'Mae and Ira', Excerpt from For the Heart of Your Soul, Sandra Jackson, PJ's Publishing, 2000

121. Good Morning America, segment on laughter as medicine, 2007

127. McDonald's jingle: "You deserve a break today, so get up and get away, to McDonald's." Service mark of McDonalds

Burden Basket: A Native American (Apache) basket hung on the door of living quarters to collect visitors' complaints and guard the privacy of the home.

Contact Information

Visit our Web site at: www.pjpublishing.org

You can also contact the publisher or author at:

pjpublishing@comcast.net

or by mail at:

P.O. Box 1396

Saugus, MA 01906

Thank you
PJ's Publishing, a division of PJKELLY & Associates
Books You Want to Read!